FEARLESS

*Become Lion-Hearted and Face Life's
Fiercest Battles Victoriously*

FEARLESS

Become Lion-Hearted and Face Life's Fiercest Battles Victoriously

By

Gemma Borbon, Emmanuel Borbon,
Leslie Bower, Kenneth Jao,
Maria Theresa Trono-Legiralde,
Jackie Lansangan-Morey, James R. Morey,
Mildred Osias, Rev. Dante Eleazar Simon

Copyright © 2021 by Customer Strategy Academy and © 2021 Jackie Morey

ALL RIGHTS RESERVED. This book contains material protected under International and Federal Laws and Treaties. Any unauthorized reprint or use of this material is prohibited. No portion of this book may be used, reproduced, stored in a retrieval system, or transmitted in any form or by any means — electronic, mechanical, photocopy, recording, scanning, or other — without express written permission from the authors or publisher, except for a brief quotation in critical reviews or articles. It is illegal to copy this book, post it to a website, or distribute it by any other means without permission from the authors and publisher.

Published by

Customer Strategy Academy, LLC

16212 Bothell Everett Hwy, Suite F111, Mill Creek, WA 98012

Publisher Jackie Morey's email: CustomerStrategyAcademy@gmail.com

Copyright Use and Public Information

Unless otherwise noted, images have been used according to public information laws.

ISBN: **978-1-7332501-7-7** Paperback

Limits of Liability and Disclaimer of Warranty

The authors and publisher shall not be liable for the reader's misuse of this material. This book is for strictly informational and educational purposes.

Scripture quotations taken from the New American Standard Bible® (NASB), Copyright © 1960, 1962, 1963, 1968, 1971, 1972, 1973, 1975, 1977, 1995 by The Lockman Foundation Used by permission. www.Lockman.org. The Holy Bible, English Standard Version® (ESV®) Copyright © 2001 by Crossway, a publishing ministry of Good News Publishers. All rights reserved. Scriptures marked NLT are taken from the HOLY BIBLE, NEW LIVING TRANSLATION (NLT): Scriptures taken from the HOLY BIBLE, NEW LIVING TRANSLATION, Copyright© 1996, 2004, 2007 by Tyndale House Foundation. Used by permission of Tyndale House Publishers, Inc., Carol Stream, Illinois 60188. All rights reserved. Used by permission. Scriptures marked NKJV are taken from the NEW KING JAMES VERSION (NKJV): Scripture taken from the NEW KING JAMES VERSION®. Copyright© 1982 by Thomas Nelson, Inc. Used by permission. All rights reserved. Scriptures marked NIV are taken from the NEW INTERNATIONAL VERSION (NIV): Scripture taken from THE HOLY BIBLE, NEW INTERNATIONAL VERSION ®. Copyright© 1973, 1978, 1984, 2011 by Biblica, Inc.™. Used by permission of Zondervan.

Disclaimer

The views expressed are those of the authors and do not reflect the official policy or position of the publisher or Customer Strategy Academy. This publication is designed to provide accurate and authoritative information regarding the subject matter covered. It is sold with the understanding that the publisher is not engaged in rendering legal, accounting, clinical or other professional advice. If legal advice or other expert assistance is required, the services of a competent professional should be sought. The opinions expressed by the authors in this book are not endorsed by Customer Strategy Academy, and are the sole responsibility of the author rendering the opinion.

DEDICATION AND ACKNOWLEDGEMENTS

Gemma Borbon – To the broken, wounded and torn who in deep torment physical and mental bear the pain, loneliness and scars - you are indeed my inspiration in humbly sharing my own journey from fear to freedom. Allow me to dedicate this to you and tell you that you are loved and not alone.

I give my heartfelt thanks to my awesome husband Noel, my children Jon and Jen, my siblings - most especially Susan who shared Jesus' saving grace, my sister in-law Mildred who I always look up to, my doctor friend Rhima Gonzaga and all my amazing friends near and far.

To the Lover of my soul King Jesus, I'm forever grateful!

Noel Borbon – To my son Jonathan Lemuel
"God has given" is the name that you bear
A fine young man you have grown in His care
To a world filled with longing
You're God's gift in belonging
Let your life touch a heart
You do know it's your part

"Devoted to God" also are you called
As the day passes by I can see it unfold
In God's field you have labored

By His grace you're consoled
Facing fear in its breadth
In your heart He is strength

Leslie Bower – To my dear "sacred sistas'" who are supporting me from heaven: Jakki MacLean and Ruth Wise.

Kenneth Jao– I would like to thank Ms. Jackie Morey and Judge Amifaith Fider-Reyes for their patience, trust and assistance. I would like to dedicate my work to those who are afraid and uncertain. This is my 1997….

Maria Theresa Trono-Legiralde – This book is dedicated to God, my Savior and Lord, who has given me this desire to write of His awesome deeds in my life. Each story will serve as memorial stones or stones of remembrance of His awesome deeds. Personal encounters or some people call it my "God-moments" and God's miraculous interventions, that reveals that God is very much involved in our lives, even the minutest detail, that He loves us and has our highest good in His heart.

And to my parents, who raised us with the knowledge and reverence of God. To my brothers and sisters, who in their own personal lives, I continue to witness God's goodness, as each of them walks in God's grace.

Special mention to my sister Jo, who has been my shoulder to cry on, my prayer partner, my confidante.

To my children, who are the generation I pass on stories of my journey with God with the prayer that they, too, will come to know and love God each passing day.

To my closest friends and mentors, who have always been there to listen to my life stories and encouraged me to live out the desire God has placed in my heart – Anna, Doreen, Wendy. Thank you for your prayers and a listening heart.

Then the LORD answered me and said: "Write the vision, and make it plain on tablets, that he may run who reads it." Habakkuk 2:2

Jackie Lansangan-Morey – I dedicate this book to the fearless ones in the persecuted Ekklesias all around the world, to the martyrs who were fearless and undaunting in their faith in Christ Jesus, and to all our spiritual fathers and mothers of the faith. I also dedicate this book to my fearless Husband Jim, our children Michael and Alyssa, to my dear friend Sharon who has interceded and fervently prayed for me and my family for about 7 years now.

I'd like to acknowledge and give all the glory to Abba Yahweh, Yeshua Ha Maschiach, and Ruach Hakodesh – Who continue to lavish their love, wisdom, revelation, and insight upon me, and Who continue to train and empower me to be fearless in any circumstance. Indeed, the best is yet to come.

James R. Morey – I'd like to acknowledge our friends and relatives for their deep love, thoughtfulness, care, lavish generosity, financial support, the prepared-and-delivered meals, supernatural prayers, emotional support, physical help, gift cards, and so much more. Thank you very much for all that you've invested into me and my family. I dedicate this book to all of you.

Mildred Osias – I dedicate this book to my grandchildren, who are loved before they are born. Reap the blessings of your ancestors' fearless obedience to God.

Rev. Dante Eleazar Simon – I dedicate this book to my wife Vively and three sons, David, Stephen and Dante Jr.

My father Dante Pelagioe Simon who taught me how to play basketball the right way and analyze the game, and my mother Brenda who instilled in us the importance of education humility and the fear of the Lord.

My siblings aka Magnificent Seven – Kuya Jojo, Elzar Dodjie, Christine Joy, Jay and Jan and Mark and myself – may our tribe increase.

TABLE OF CONTENTS

Foreword		1
Chapter 1:	Journey from Fear to Freedom	3
Chapter 2:	Strength of Heart	29
Chapter 3:	She Looks to the Future and Smiles!	45
Chapter 4:	Nil Desperandum!	59
Chapter 5:	It All Began	71
Chapter 6:	7 Deadly Fears and How to Overcome Them	95
Chapter 7:	A Leg to Stand On	133
Chapter 8:	Fearless to Soar and Shine	157
Chapter 9:	Fearless Faith	183
Afterword		203

FOREWORD

A somewhat unconventional drawcard to be talking about fear. But the reality is that everyone struggles, or has struggled with one or more forms of it in their lifetime. Some of you may be going through this very adversity right now.

Some fears are minor and somewhat laughable like the fear of spiders. Others are very real and debilitating like the fear of heights, or the fear of strangers. Others are deep-seated, less apparent but potentially more impacting, like the fear of failure, rejection or death.

This book, written by nine authors with a combined experience of close to five centuries have something worthwhile to say about this topic. I am privileged to say that I personally know five of them and can attest to their wisdom and pilgrimage.

There is power, certainly truth, in lived-through stories. This is such a book. It is filled with authentic experiences. It can be raw at times. I think that's when it serves as a mirror to ourselves. We all need that, to firstly realize that we are not alone in our struggles. And hopefully in that realization, you will find something in these chapters to hold on to to help you battle through your own encounters with fear to emerge victorious at the other end.

Here are just some of the headliner topics that I gleaned to be the most relevant that you will find particularly useful:

Identifying and acknowledging fear
Prescriptions for dealing with fear
Lessons while navigating through battle
Where to draw strength

You will find that in all these, it is that these writers went through life *not fearlessly,* but rather, that they have learned to *fear less.* And this can give us the confidence that we need that we too, can do the same.

Thank you to Jackie Lansangan-Morey, international best-selling author herself and one of the contributing writers of this book for the privilege of writing this foreword.

Aleli Grace Angeles-Corpuz

International Bestselling Collaborative Author of

"Divinely Designed: How to Surrender to the Potter's Hand, Go Through the Fires and Crises of Life and Become His Masterpiece" and "Unstoppable: How to Successfully Tackle Life's Obstacles and Thrive"

CHAPTER 1
JOURNEY FROM FEAR TO FREEDOM
By Gemma Borbon

Where Is That Girl?

"*I Miss My Real Self! Where is that girl who was like Wonder Woman? As soon as she hits the ground, the devil is already shaking – the child of God and princess prayer warrior is up. She is energetic, passionate, happy, bubbly, courageous, positive and a risk-taker!*

I noticed that early this year, my emotions were like a roller coaster – up and down, up and down – but mostly down. I must literally talk myself into moving and being happy; otherwise, I will just stay in bed, sad, crying, and without motivation to work at all.

This is insane because I am a wife, a mother, an employee, a leader, and a Pastor's wife. I need to get up early to cook for my family, drop my husband off at the train station and still do household chores all before going to work. I do not like what I have become.

I know myself, and I am not like this. This is not me at all! The family probably wonders, but no one has asked me yet. I am doing my best to still function well and wear a smile every day; it is exceedingly difficult. I am a totally different person. Sometimes I'll be super happy; then my mood would suddenly change."

That was the opening to an email I sent to my best friend on December 20, 2016.

I finished my certificate in Bookkeeping and Financial Services in 1999. That was when I suffered tendonitis on my left ankle, and my youngest daughter was only around 20 months old at that time. My condition left me limping at the expense of my other foot, that it, too, started to swell.

One morning, my husband woke up to me urgently crawling in excruciation. Shocked, he immediately picked me up and carried me to the wheelchair to which I had been bound for over three months.

When I thought it could not get any worse, my knee also started to swell to the point that my specialist had to drain water out of it, and then inject steroids. I remember how petrified I was when my specialist rang me to discuss the results from the plethora of blood tests, x-rays, and screenings.

What is wrong with me, Lord? What more or what else could go wrong?

I was *so* terrified I could hardly move, and the pounding of my heart deafened my doctor's discussion. I was so nervous that I *thought* I heard the diagnosis as HIV. How on earth would I get that?

I had been serving the Lord joyfully and faithfully. I read my bible, prayed, and did my quiet time daily. It was as if my mind refused to process the diagnosis at the time until I went to my General Practitioner.

My doctor explained that there were a hundred different types of arthritis and related conditions, but I only knew two

– osteoarthritis and gout. I had seronegative arthritis and an autoimmune disorder where my antibodies were attacking the good cells in my joints, and if not controlled, could attack my organs as well.

I was a healthy and active person and yet I had seronegative arthritis?! It did not make sense! I was totally devastated and **fearful** as I did not understand what was going on with my body.

I wept and cried to the Lord, prayed for His help and mercy, asked for His healing, strength, and deliverance just like King David did when he prayed through his fears and pains in Psalms.

I desperately looked for God's promises in His word that I could intensely cling on to. God is a rewarder of those who honestly seek Him. He led me to read the following scriptures:

Exodus 23:25 "Worship the Lord your God, and his blessing will be on your food and water. I will take away sickness from among you."

Psalm 107:20 "He sent out his word and healed them; he rescued them from the grave."

Psalm 118:17 "I will not die but live, and will proclaim what the LORD has done."

Malachi 4:2 "But to you who fear My name The Sun of Righteousness shall arise with healing in His wings, And you shall go out And grow fat like stall-fed calves."

This was God's instruction to the Israelites to serve and worship the Lord who had brought them out of Egypt. He had done so many great and good things for them at the Red

Sea and in the Wilderness, and as they obeyed, He blessed their bread and water. I believe the scriptures to be true and living. And with all my heart, I began praying and declaring His words *daily*.

I hold on to these until now. I also prophesied these words over my body, my immune system, and my organs. I declared the blood of Jesus running through my veins. These verses became my life's verses.

Worship Leader, Wonder Woman and a Juggler

My close friends at church call me Wonder Woman and a Juggler as they witness how active my life is and how I balanced my family life with my ministry.

No one and nothing could ever stop me from serving Him, not even in my last term of pregnancy. I was still dancing and jumping around and praising Him with passion and exuberance. My infant and toddler kids, sickness and health condition could not hinder me. I still served the Lord with gladness – led the congregation to worship Him in spirit and truth. *"Serve the LORD with gladness and delight; Come before His presence with joyful singing." Psalm 100:2 (AMP)*

I still worshipped and praised my Awesome God and Savior from my innermost being even when I was in the wheelchair. *I will praise You, O Lord my God, with all my heart, And I will glorify Your name forevermore. Psalm 86:12 NKJV.*

Candidly, being in a wheelchair for three months hindered me from fully expressing my worship and adoration in dance and movement.

My husband was one of the pastors of our previous church, the "Love of Jesus Christian Ministry." I served and worked alongside him. We were partners in the ministry side-by-side.

We believe that when God called him to be a pastor, I, too, was called because we are one, although our gifts and roles are different and unique from each other.

"We have different gifts, according to the grace given to each of us. If your gift is prophesying, then prophesy in accordance with your faith; if it is serving, then serve; if it is teaching, then teach; if it is to encourage, then give encouragement; if it is giving, then give generously; if it is to lead, do it diligently; if it is to show mercy, do it cheerfully." Romans 12:6-8 NIV

We are one, but we maintain and respect our individuality. I was the head of the Praise and Worship Ministry and a Prayer Watch Coordinator for three years, liaising with pastors and leaders of different churches. This was in response to our Senior Pastor responding to the call of God to gather churches in our city for seven years to pray for our nation, family and community.

I was actively involved in different ministries, so I learned to manage and balance my time for family, church, and work. I recognize the specific gift and calling that God had placed on our lives and had anointed us to do. When He called us, He also empowered us. *Hebrews 13:21 NIV "Now may the God of peace…equip you with everything good for doing his will, and may he work in us what is pleasing to him, through Jesus Christ, to whom be glory for ever and ever. Amen."* **Praise the Lord!**

I Miss The Real Me!

Everything had changed, and I almost didn't recognize myself!

It was in 2011 when I was diagnosed with Rheumatoid Arthritis (RA), Hypothyroidism and Type 2 diabetes. All were related to my autoimmune health issue. I have been on strong medication for my RA and thyroid since then. My doctor had to check my liver function, kidney, blood count, ESR and CRP measures for RA every three months; every six months whenever I felt a lot better. Thank God that my blood sugars are under control through diet and exercise.

I totally asked God for His mercy. I told God that I didn't want to take another medication. Miraculously, God heard my prayers!! I am also very grateful to Him for the privilege He has given me to live in one of the most generous countries in the world where our health system is excellent, and I don't need to pay for all my tests and my GP (General Practitioner) consultation. Our government is very helpful to all permanent residents and Australian citizens, especially those with chronic disease.

In 2016, I suffered depression, which I previously mentioned in my email. I was not even aware of it until I went to my GP in 2018. I was in denial since I had been a pastor's wife, a leader, a wife and a mother. I totally did not pay attention to all the signs that flagged every day.

In my mind, I needed to be strong all the time for my family and others. I needed to stay composed, look ok and vibrant. I am by nature an encourager, an exhorter who finds joy in encouraging people. Others said that it is a gift from God. So, I could not afford to be sad in front of others and be a cause of their disappointment and discouragement. I tried so hard with my own effort to be happy.

I also had this notion that I thought depression always had something to do with demonic forces, so I had to be careful not to let others see what was inside me.

What would others possibly think? I had been Spirit-filled and was a prayer warrior. I refused the idea of depression happening to me. I adamantly denied it, and I ignored it. I was *fearful* of disappointing my family, friends and the church.

I also didn't know about the menopausal problem, chemical imbalance, and other disadvantages of my autoimmune problem until I was going downhill and felt like going deeper into the pit.

My Daughter's Response and my Son's Reactions

Finally, I spoke to my daughter about it.

I showed the email to her and let her read it as I didn't know how to open up the topic.

I have always been grateful for my beautiful relationship with my two children, where we can talk about anything under the sun. I am not just a mother to them, but I am also their best friend.

My daughter cried and hugged me after she finished reading my email. She prayed for me, showed love, compassion and understanding.

She faithfully stood up for me and became my arbiter when her brother and I, or sometimes their dad and I, disagreed – especially when it turned into a heated discussion, and I would be out of line and out of control.

There were many instances outside our home that my daughter would volunteer to talk to the person, teller, or anyone who would cross me.

One fateful day, I remember screaming at a person while waiting in the queue to go into the movie theater! My son was so upset and felt totally embarrassed when I was furious, because I shouted at the girl and insulted her to go back to her own country, forgetting that I myself was also a foreigner who did not grow up in Australia.

I reacted badly to her comment because she mistakenly thought I was trying to go in before her. Although I noticed she was the same girl in front of me while buying the tickets, she gave me a nasty look when I accidentally bumped her shoulder despite apologizing to her.

I remember it all so vividly – my daughter Jennifer asked her brother gently to stop explaining how rude, out of control and very cross I was. She was trying to appease her brother and asked him to understand me. She then proceeded to console me.

My son is a kindhearted person and compassionate. He was simply embarrassed by my intense and fierce reaction, which I understood after I reflected on it.

I missed the real me!

The person who had been perfectly created in God's image. *Then God said, "Let Us make man in Our image, according to Our likeness; Genesis 1:26a NKJV.*

What happened to that bubbly, happy and funny woman? It felt like God's perfect creation was locked inside. The song of Casting Crown "Who Am I," described who I was at that time.

WHO AM I?

The song "Who Am I" by Casting Crowns profoundly expresses how I've felt during this time...

Go to this link for the lyrics and tune:
https://youtu.be/3rT8Re1EIQc

Who am I? Whose am I? What is my identity?

I was broken. I lost myself. I didn't know who I was anymore. I needed help. My GP referred me to a psychologist, and I began seeing her regularly. We became friends. She is a Christian and so lovely.

During my first meeting, I remember it was awkward, and I was teary, but the knowledge of her being a Christian gave me peace and removed my awkwardness. I ended up praying with her before I left her office.

I felt somehow we connected, established trust and friendship. My first meeting with my psychologist was incredible and unforgettable. I had been betrayed, misinterpreted and rejected many times, and it was not easy for me to trust anyone. At that time, I always thought from a perspective of self-preservation; but in that room, I opened myself up and became vulnerable, trusting her with my brokenness, sadness, pain, and story.

I told her my family background being the youngest among ten siblings. I was so open, that I even mentioned my brother who took his own life because of depression when I was in my senior year. I was 15 years old when I was summoned to the principal's office and was told of the bad news – my brother was forever gone. It was his second attempt after the first one, which wasn't successful. I did not fully understand why my brother took his own life because everyone loved him. He was kind, caring, sweet and funny.

God's Love Saw Me – From Nothing to Something, From Rejected to Accepted

I was loved by my mother and believed to be her favorite, being the youngest but not my father's choice. His favorite was my older sister. I was very competitive in my younger years at school. I studied hard and was very active in extracurricular activities. I felt the need for approval to be loved and accepted, so I did my best to excel academically, and in everything I engaged myself in.

I grew up believing I was ugly and adopted because I didn't look like my siblings. They teased me that I was the daughter of our neighbor. I have darker skin, while my siblings are fair-skinned. I was insecure and arrogant. I was very proud of my achievements as I graduated with honors and high recognition. I had low self-esteem, but I was a strong-willed, ambitious, high achiever and idealistic person.

My siblings disliked me because of my attitude. They had told my story to friends, comparing me to my other sister. They said that I was opinionated and had a know-it-all personality. I answered back at them.

I was hypersensitive, and I despised correction. I was defensive and had reasons for everything I did wrong. I also loved showing off my talents to get attention.

Negative remarks and comments impaired my self-esteem. My poor identity was marred by what my siblings have defined me. I felt unloved and rejected. I believed what they had tagged me, the "ugly," "adopted," and conceited girl during my formative years to adulthood. I began to believe that I was not good enough! I felt insignificant and less valued, so I always tried hard to be competent and accomplished.

When I came to know Jesus and have a personal relationship with Him, I found my true identity. His love saw me, and what my sibling have defined me, He transformed. His love accepts and restores. His love found me!

"But you are a chosen generation, a royal priesthood, a holy nation, His own special people, that you may proclaim the praises of Him who called you out of darkness into His marvelous light;" 1 Peter 2:9 NKJV

I am His masterpiece. I am loved. I am chosen. I am a princess daughter of the King. His blood runs through my veins. I have His DNA. Praise the Lord!

I am a chosen race! God chose me.

John 15:16, "You did not choose me, but I chose you….," Ephesians 1:4a "…..just as He chose us in Him before the foundation of the world."

I am His masterpiece.

Ephesians 2:10, "*For we are His workmanship, created in Christ Jesus for good works, which God prepared beforehand so that we would walk in them.*"

You see, I was made for Him and I was chosen to declare His praises. Declaring His greatness not just by mere words but also by our lifestyle – is the reason for our very existence. We were created to love Him. And when we praise and worship Him as our response to His love, we fulfill His purpose.

He has called us out of *darkness* – from a meaningless life, marred by sin, hurtful behaviors, and wrong motivations, into a purposeful life, to experience His marvelous light.

We are special people because we belong to Him. We are chosen for the high calling of priestly work. We are set apart to do His works. Believe it or not, we are a royal priesthood. Hallelujah!

We have access to Him any time of the day without getting an appointment to meet and talk to Him. We can come to Him just as we are! I like the Message translation of 1 Peter 2:9-10 MSG *"But you are the ones chosen by God, chosen for the high calling of priestly work, chosen to be a holy people, God's instruments to do his work and speak out for him, to tell others of the night-and-day difference he made for you—from nothing to something, from rejected to accepted."*

My God Encounter During a Magnificent, Mellow Sunset

It was during a school holiday when I accepted Jesus in my heart as my personal Lord and Savior on top of the roof of our bungalow house when my sister shared the love of God and led me to a prayer of acceptance.

It was in the late afternoon when the sky looked like a canvas as the sun was setting down. The sunset was merely a prelude to the dawn. While sitting on top of the roof watching the sunset after praying, my heart was filled with the majesty of His presence. The assurance of His love wrapped around me, and hope was born, that tomorrow would come with a promise of a beautiful new day and unfailing mercy.

After the school holiday, as we went back to Manila, my sister invited me to MLQ University (Manuel L. Quezon University) where they would hold their fellowship and worship service in Mandaluyong City. She taught me how to pray, and she has been my encourager and my prayer partner. She was amazed as she witnessed my transformation. God had changed me from the inside out, from glory to glory. *"Therefore, if anyone is in Christ, he is a new creation; the old has passed away; behold, the new has come!"* [2 Corinthians 5:17 ESV]

I became a follower of Christ at the age of 16.

I started to share my personal encounter with Christ, and my faith with my classmates. I regularly attended my sister's fellowship until my classmate told me about a Christian fellowship and bible study at the chapel where I was studying at Polytechnic University of the Philippines (PUP). I checked it out and was grateful for my classmates.

They knew I was a born-again Christian. They accepted the Lord, too. Though I was still a baby Christian, I was able to help and encourage them to grow in their faith and follow Christ.

I was mentored at the Power of God Church and actively involved in different ministries, namely: Tribe of Judah Choir, Acts 4:31 Singing Group, I was a worship leader and a member of praise and worship ministry, I was a small group bible study leader in a slum area, camp counselor and program coordinator, and an assistant leader in the young professionals' group.

I was one of the presidents of one of their campus ministries at PUP, where I was finishing my degree and at another underground campus at CEU (Centro Escolar University).

I supported other different schools and universities whenever I was needed. I was committed and dedicated. My studies were never an excuse for me not to serve and be passionate in my service to the Lord.

Having a personal relationship and encounter with God is the best thing that has ever happened to me.

Incredible, Incomprehensible, Infinite, Immeasurable His Love Is!

Psalm 8 NIV

A psalm of David. *Lord, our Lord, how majestic is your name in all the earth! You have set your glory in the heavens. Through the praise of children and infants you have established a stronghold against your enemies, to silence the foe and the avenger. When I consider your heavens, the work of your fingers, the moon and the stars, which you have set in place, what is mankind that you are mindful of them, human beings that you care for them? You have made the a little lower than the angels and crowned them with glory and honor. You made them rulers over the works of your hands; you put everything under their feet: all flocks and herds, and the animals of the wild, the birds in the sky, and the fish in the sea, all that swim the paths of the seas. Lord, our Lord, how majestic is your name in all the earth*!

How could a Majestic God, the Creator of the universe deeply love someone – a frail, tiny, insignificant and sinful creature like me?

How could He, the most powerful infinite Being whose Name is Excellent, Magnificent, Supreme, Glorious, Splendid and Majestic in all the Earth that even heavens cannot contain His glory, love me personally? Yet He cares deeply about me. He is mindful of me and visited me. His love is incredible, indescribable, infinite, immeasurable and unfailing.

His love never runs out. His perfect love drives out fear. *"There is no fear in love, but perfect love casts out fear. For fear has to do with punishment, and whoever fears has not been perfected in love."* 1 John 4:18 ESV.

During my worst days as the dark was approaching, I remember that driving back home was sickening because memories of my childhood and my loved ones, most especially my beloved mother's memory, began to flood my mind. I missed her so much. I remember moments in the past, sad and hurtful events, people, and places that made me sad, and I couldn't help but sob and cry.

I was overwhelmed with grief and sadness as memories of disappointments, rejections and past hurts caused by people I deeply loved and cared about filled my mind.

Going to sleep gave me anxiety because I knew I would wake up so early the following day with a feeling of despair, grief, and indescribable sadness.

I felt so broken that I couldn't understand why it was happening. I felt so dead inside with no hope and purpose for living. I was so afraid of what I would do to end all those negative emotions as suicidal thoughts started to creep into me.

It was horrible thinking of the grief, separation, pain and desolation my children would feel if I were to take my life. It broke my heart and brought me tears thinking about it.

I was so adamant about sharing with my family what exactly was going on in my mind because I didn't want to worry them. But I was also *fearful* of being judged and misunderstood. I didn't want to hear any advice on what to do and not to do. I didn't even want them to quote scriptures just to comfort me because it didn't make sense, and I already knew it, maybe not all of it but at least some of it.

I was aware of the effects on my physical body. I knew what to do, but I did not have the strength and capacity to apply it. I fully recognized that those negative emotions were not true at all.

I tried to hide and fight so hard. Prayed so hard, and read my bible regularly. I joined online teaching and bible studies about depression with Sheila Walsh, Rebekah Lyons and Dr. Caroline Leaf. I even listened to their podcasts and bought their books.

I tried to occupy my time with lots of activities, though it was not easy; it was so difficult and almost impossible to move every day. I seriously needed a miracle! I had to choose to get up, dress up and do my usual routine.

NEVER ALONE

My husband was indeed a gift from God. He was so loving and very supportive. He would do anything and was willing to give me anything within his means just to make me happy. We traveled a lot, two sometimes three times a year, holidaying overseas – Europe, Emirates and Asia.

We went out regularly every week for a date in the city, ate at different restaurants and rode a boat around Sydney CBD (Central Business District), watching and enjoying the sky, Harbor Bridge and the Opera House.

The love of my family and few special friends kept me going. I know other people probably cannot believe it because there was no trace of fear, anxiety, and depression outside my home. The extravagant and perfect love of God casts out my fears. It has protected me. His love that wrapped around me was my shield against the darts of toxic emotions. The promise of His loving presence and that I was not and will never be alone on those dark and lonely nights have been my anchor and light.

Jesus, the TRUTH overpowered the lies of darkness and gave me hope. The Majestic Name of Jesus silences my depression and anxiety. The amazing, unconditional, unstoppable and incomprehensible love of God expels my fears.

REST, CONNECT AND RECOVER

Rest

I am still on the journey. Currently, my job was temporarily closed down because of financial loss. I worked for a Non-Profit organization. Prior to the temporary business close down, three permanent staff positions were considered redundant. I must admit that my workplace was one of unhealthy contributing factors to my mental health.

My husband's position was also declared redundant before the Covid-19 pandemic even happened for one and a half years. Since August 2019, I have been the sole breadwinner for our family. I could not resign and look for another job for that reason. I also feel that God still has a purpose for my stay.

It has been two months since my work had been shut down temporarily, although I still have some responsibilities to help the management (composed of ten volunteer board of directors).

I was asked to report to work once a week, sometimes twice, as needed. I mainly stayed at home in my garden. It was also a blessing anyway, because I needed a rest.

God actually answered my prayers, not according to what I envisioned. *"For as the heavens are higher than the earth, So are My ways higher than your ways, And My thoughts than your thoughts. Isaiah 55:9 KJV*

The best part is I get to rest.

Rest is one of the spiritual disciplines that is often taught but rarely applied. Rest is essential to our spiritual walk with the Lord, and many don't appreciate its value. Rest allows our mind, body, and soul to renew and start with even more strength, focus and vitality.

The analogy that I could think of is a computer. Sometimes a program or application in the computer encounters an error, and the software hangs. Restarting the system will refresh the applications.

These scriptures rejuvenated and refreshed me…

"Be still before the LORD and wait patiently for him" Psalm 37:7 NIV

"But those who wait on the Lord Shall renew their strength; They shall mount up with wings like eagles, They shall run and not be weary, They shall walk and not faint." Isaiah 40:31NKJV

God indeed is inviting us to rest.

Connect

Now I have time to connect and bond again with my friends physically and virtually. I have many awesome friends that I treasure and consider God's gift from above. My GP is one of them. I want to mention this because her impact on my life was tremendous. She is an amazing, godly woman who is very close to my heart, a special friend and a sister in Christ who helps me a lot in this journey of fear, depression and anxiety to healing, restoration and freedom.

She was like a beacon of light during my darkest hours. She saw to it that she called me before and after work. She sometimes stopped work between patients to check up on me and pray, even on the phone. She has a busy, hectic schedule, and many friends. I am grateful that I have the privilege to be one of them.

Friendships are important. *"Sweet friendships refresh the soul and awaken our hearts with joy, for good friends are like the anointing oil that yields the fragrant incense of God's presence." Proverbs 27:9 TPT*

Recover

Learning a new thing this year is pretty cool and amazing. God has given us many gifts and talents that we should always endeavor to improve and discover.

This year, I started gardening! The covid-19 restriction was not a lockdown for me but a time to redirect my focus from self to something. I wanted to try and learn a new thing. I discovered that gardening is therapeutic. True enough, watching my plants and vegetables grow and thrive gives me so much happiness and hope.

The best part is that the God of the universe, which earth is His footstool and heaven is His throne, speaks to me through my plants, veggies, and flowers. He is very personal and loves communicating with His children, and reveals Who He is in many ways.

He is my Divine Master Gardener, and I am His flower. I learned that to be able to care for your plants properly - so that they will live, grow, flower and bear fruits, you need to know their names, their needs, how much water they need, what soil to use, and how much exposure to sunlight they need. Some need full sunlight and others are to be partly-shaded. They need nutrients, so you give them fertilizers.

The location of plants and their origins are also important. Some plants are challenging, and some are easy to care for.

It is exciting to watch their growth every day. There are many varieties, but some are unique. We prevent pests from infiltrating them. You treat them when your plant is sick. Our Great God does the same even more remarkably because He gave His life for us to save, heal and give us eternal life. He knows our names, even the numbers of our hairs. He cares so much about us. He wants us to grow and bear fruits.

He takes pleasure in us and rejoices over us with singing. *"The LORD your God among you is powerful – he will save, and he will take joyful delight in you. In his love he will renew you with his love; he will celebrate with singing because of you."* Zephaniah 3:17 ISV

We all have stories to tell.

We experience universal pain, whether physical, mental or emotional, but we are *never* alone. God has been so good and faithful to us. He is our faithful friend and companion. He promised that He would never leave us nor forsake us.

My depression, fear and anxiety drew me closer to God. I learned to trust Him fully.

I still experience pain in my body and feel sadness from time to time, but I am *free from fears!*

I learned to pray through my fears and pain. You see, the Lover of my soul is real. His love has kept me and preserved me. Nothing can separate me from His love. And God is so amazing that nothing is wasted in His Kingdom. Even in our suffering, pain and brokenness, He can still use us for His glory.

I have read that the most beautiful souls are often the most broken.

To God be the glory, honor and power forever. Amen!

Before I end with a prayer from my heart that's based on God's word, here's a beautiful version of portion of "The Lord's Prayer"…

"Our Beloved Father, dwelling in the heavenly realms, may the glory of your name be the center on which our lives turn. Manifest your kingdom realm, and cause your every purpose to be fulfilled on earth, just as it is fulfilled in heaven." Matthew 6:9-10 TPT

Prayer

Dear God, our Heavenly Father, You are our Great Shepherd, we have everything that we need because you always provide. You let us rest in green pastures and lead us beside quiet waters. You renew our strength and guide us along right paths for your name's sake. Even when we walk through the valley of death, we are not to be afraid for you are close beside us, your rod and your staff protect and comfort us. It is you who directs our steps. I pray that you will lead us to the right paths giving honor to your name. (based on Psalm 23)

Abba Father, You are our Great Healer. I pray for your healing balm for all those who are sick of covid-19, other types of illnesses and lingering diseases. Let your resurrection power bring wellness within and restoration to their entire being.

I lift up those who are in pain, broken hearted and suffering from mental illness, depression, fear, panic attack and anxiety. Lord, you are a miracle worker and a promise keeper. May they find new hope in you Jesus. You are the fountain of life. Please pour down your life giving water upon them. I pray that you breathe life and hope into their wounded and anxious soul. Will you heal and carry them through. Let them feel the love and comfort of your presence. In Jesus' Mighty Name. Amen!

L→R: Gem's son Jonathan, husband Noel, Gem, and daughter Jen

GEMMA BORBON

Gemma Borbon is a worship leader and a prayer warrior at West Sydney Community Church. She is very passionate in encouraging and mentoring the young people of her local church having been mentored herself during her younger years in Power of God Fellowship in the Philippines.

She is actively involved in prayer and intercession ministry at Love of Jesus Christian Ministries. She loves exhorting and encouraging others as God gives the opportunity.

She earned her degree in Engineering at the Polytechnic University of the Philippines. She worked in the telecommunications industry for five years prior to migrating to Australia on August 1991.

She married Noel the following year and started their life together in Sydney. They share the blessing, love and faith of son Jonathan and daughter Jennifer.

CHAPTER 2
STRENGTH OF HEART
By Emmanuel Borbon

THE BOY IN THE DARK

Yea, though I walk through the valley of the shadow of death, I will fear no evil: for thou art with me; thy rod and thy staff they comfort me.

Psalm 23:4 (KJV)

The young teenager stood frozen in ambivalence before taking his first step. It didn't help at all feeling the humidity of that summer night. It would have been a generous relief to feel even just a brief cold breeze sweep across his face.

It was one second before midnight. Then ding-dong – the hands struck twelve. He started walking with trepidation as he plunged into the darkness. Save the feint illumination offered by minute glimpses of light, it was not easy to navigate his way. He was halfway along the path when, without a moment's notice, everything changed. The courage he had as he took his first step started to fade away. As the darkness became more prominent, an uncomfortable douse of unpleasant feeling invaded his heart, mind and soul. Absence of light took its course on ebb and the boy's unpleasant feelings transported its way into his physical body. The sense between hot and cold wouldn't tarry as it swung endlessly like a pendulum in a wall clock. Tremor in his arms and hands partnered with his legs that gave in to feebleness.

The neutral impression of ambivalence he first had shifted and leaned towards the dark, mysterious, threatening side – panic, horror, and terror – FEAR – unrelenting. Could he move on? Could he take another step; more steps to complete the journey? Must he do this alone?

I think of the many occasions feelings of fear had crippled me. It's like pain that's almost unbearable or paralysis at its utmost! The most common response is to hide or run away towards the opposite direction.

One can't help imagine the opportunities missed, fun relinquished, adventures abandoned, ventures forfeited, pleasures deprived of, potentials unfulfilled, mountain peaks unconquered, dreams unfulfilled, love lost and far worse a destiny one never collided with and in its deepest sense perhaps a life never lived. I couldn't word it more succinctly than Daniel Kolenda's book title – "Live Before You Die."

There is this game called "Two Truths and a Lie." Often the game is played as an ice-breaker and usually effective with people who have just met for the first time or have known each other only for a short time. There is no set number of players in the game. Each participant takes a turn to mention something about himself which consists of two statements of truth and one statement which is a lie. The rest of the people in the group then guess which of the three statements is the lie. Consider for example the following statements about me:

- I have reached the summit of Mount Sinai in 2018
- I received a commission of Lieutenant in the Philippine Army
- I have a birthmark on my right leg

One of the statements above is a lie.

Some skillful individuals are good at this and can work out the lie statement based on sentence construction and the person's body language. I guess, the more you play the game the more you become adept at learning to cover the single lie among the two truths. And this is valid even among people who have known each other for long.

Sometimes I wonder if we do live life like this game.

Do we justify and say that at least the amount of truth surpasses the lie and it should be fine? When God is not acknowledged as ultimate reality, then indeed life will be lived like this game. Professions of truths will not match behavior.

There is also then the subtle, hidden and more dangerous type where truth convictions are realized but because of fear, actions are sanitized and made to look as if they are born out of those convictions. Conviction does not necessarily result into right action all the time. In the game of half-truths do we succumb to fear or rise in protest to its clutches?

SELF-PRESERVATION

Then Jesus told his disciples, "If anyone would come after me, let him deny himself and take up his cross and follow me. For whoever would save his life will lose it, but whoever loses his life for my sake will find it.

Matthew 16:24-25 (ESV)

Why are we afraid?

First time fear appears in the bible is in the Garden of Eden[1]. God asked Adam, "Where are you?" Adam answered, "I heard the sound of you in the garden, and I was afraid, because I was naked, and I hid myself." God then replied, "Who told you that you were naked? Have you eaten of the tree of which I commanded you not to eat?"

The Genesis narrative tells a lot of Adam's departure from the presence of God. The healthy relationship they had with their creator turned into a historic separation from Him bringing about utter depravity for all generations to come.

Notice in the account how self-consciousness came upon Adam. All of a sudden there was a preoccupation with his nakedness. From that point, everything went south. He consequently blamed Eve ("the woman" as men would like to emphasize). Well, Adam had a very brief reprieve when God drew his attention to Eve when she was asked, "What is this that you have done?" But God's attention went back to Adam and this time clearly implying he was the one foremost responsible for his and his wife's action.

---

[1] Genesis 3

STRENGTH OF HEART

Self-consciousness became the evidence of Adam's *fear*; the *disobedience* to eat of the tree of knowledge of good and evil – was the vehicle for its inception.

Why are we afraid?

I could think of a few reasons: (1) shame, embarrassment or ridicule; (2) uncertainty or the unknown; (3) failure; (4) death or bodily harm; (5) imminent threat; (6) rejection; (7) exposure; (8) isolation or abandonment; (9) temporary or permanent loss. Surely there are thousands more. Whatever the cause or reason, fear has become part and parcel of human existence.

Some say fear is a learned behavior. Notice how children display fearless manners. They grab and taste anything, jump from whatever the height is, keep running till they bump into something, scream at anyone, cry in public, break things, throw things freely as well as a variety of other silly things.

We either get annoyed at them or laugh at how carefree, funny and amusing they are. Then they acquire more information, learn, mature and begin to develop fear for things they used to not to be afraid of.

Isn't it shocking that, sometimes, what we learn could be the very means that leads to our demise? In the New Testament the scribes and Pharisees took pride in their knowledge but how counter-intuitive was Jesus' teaching about learning in the context of a yoke – "Take my yoke upon you, and learn from me[2]."

Didn't Jesus talk about having childlike faith? Wasn't this what was expected of Adam and Eve in the Garden of Eden?

---
[2] Matthew 11:29

In their innocence, they were free to choose and trust God in everything. Sadly they chose to pay attention to the serpent and disobey God[3].

When we decide to label a thing as a *threat* it becomes an **object of fear**. The appetite for the glory of God to serve in our calling is subdued. Our pursuit for the holy vocation is replaced by retreat and seclusion into the dungeon of fear.

Very much like the Parable of the Talents, where the servant who played it safe (because he was afraid) arrived at negative consequences[4]. Calvin Miller was spot on when he wrote, "Should we not all be flexible before we know God's will? Should we not all be immovable after we understand what He wants done?[5]"

There are those who say some fears are handed down to us (genetically). That is to say we fear certain things because we have a propensity to do so. What's interesting is that in Exodus 34:6-7 (ESV), 'The Lord passed before him and proclaimed, "The Lord, the Lord, a God merciful and gracious, slow to anger, and abounding in steadfast love and faithfulness, keeping steadfast love for thousands, forgiving iniquity and transgression and sin, but who will by no means clear the guilty, visiting the iniquity of the fathers on the children and the children's children, to the third and the fourth generation."'

How complex this thing called *fear* is. The task at hand, however, is finding out how we are to be liberated from the grips of fear and soar above the clouds freely like an eagle.

---

[3] Genesis 2-3

[4] Matthew 25:14-30; Luke 19:11-27

[5] Calvin Miller, Into the Depths of God, 22

A beautiful quote from Rabbi Nachman of Breslov says, "The world is a narrow bridge and the important thing is to not be afraid.[6]" The analogy here helps a lot in framing our thinking. The problem of the narrowness is a given and the solution to overcome it is provided but the steps in applying the solution are what we need to figure out. Life in this world certainly is a walk of faith.

Why are we afraid?

I asked my daughter the same question. She answered, "Self-preservation." I asked my wife and she replied, "I love myself." This sounds a bit eerily profound.

I took some time to reflect on these and tried hard to think of all the fears I had encountered and the ones I know other people had. They all seem to be connected to *preserving self* including the fear of losing a loved one or breaking up a relationship. Even if it's a tiny bit there is a part of us we don't want to give up so we fear losing it.

Didn't Jesus say that whoever loses his life for His name's sake will save it[7]? You will find at least twenty five New Testament references to losing one's life for the sake of Christ and a few allusions to it in the Old Testament. The references on denying self, which is even more abundant, hammer the idea solidly. To deny ourselves and take up our cross surely is a fearful thing but to follow Jesus is the only true guarantee to preserving ourselves.

Why are you afraid?

---

[6] https://dailystoic.com/the-world-is-a-narrow-bridge/
[7] Mark 8:35

Jesus posed the same question[8] to his disciples when they were in the middle of a windstorm. Jesus was fast asleep and his disciples were terrified so they woke him up. Right after they drew his attention, Jesus calmed the strong wind and the raging sea.

One thing I noticed; though it was already peaceful, they were still afraid – this time not of the wind and the sea but of Jesus. Fear needs to be directed to God for the stillness to come.

When self-preservation is the agenda of life, focus on God is set aside. If we are to face our fears with courage we ought to be constantly engaged in the practice of the presence of God[9].

DRAW THE CURTAIN ONCE MORE

> *"My flesh and my heart may fail, but God is the strength of my heart and my portion forever."*
>
> ~Psalm 73:26 (ESV)

Fear appears to be an unavoidable feature of living. Somehow it is a paradox. On one hand it could render us immobile, but on the other hand it could help us become aware and thus, we pay attention to what is most important and what is of ultimate value to us.

It is the response to fear and what's done next that separates the victor from the vanquished.

In the many Bible translations I searched, the word "fearless" occurs in very rare instances on a few translations [10], Other

---

[8] Mark 4:40

[9] Brother Lawrence, The Practice of the Presence of God

translations render it as follows: without fear, having no fear, devoid of fear, has no fear, not afraid, or one that is rather quite explicit "without the ability to fear (ISV)[11]." The word "fearless" gives me the impression that it is coined in the modern era. The ancient Biblical world rather speaks of courage or literally, "strength of heart."

Have we ever thought that courage is not possible when there is no fear? The bible says that there is no fear in love; but perfect love casts out all fear[12]. Courage, I believe, is an expression of perfect love. It is the posture one takes in the presence of fear. From a Christian perspective fear could be viewed as giving attention to something or someone other than God[13]. A summon to courage is a call to look unto Jesus the author and finisher of our faith[14]. Courage comes when we face our fears. To run away from our fears is to deny ourselves of the grace God has made available for us at the moment.

In this humble existence of ours, God seems to open doors of opportunity for us to exercise courage within the covering of His love. King Solomon has been quoted as saying, "Happy is the man who is always scared.[15]""Scared" is the word translated "fear" in most Bible translations of the book of Proverbs. It refers to the "fear of the Lord." Rabbis explain it

---

[10] New Living Translation; Amplified Bible Classic Edition; Contemporary English Version; God's Word Translation

[11] International Standard Version

[12] 1 John 4:18

[13] Eric Gilmour, https://www.youtube.com/watch?v=sSEwFmYhGUM

[14] Hebrews 12:2

[15] Proverbs 28:14 (NAB 1995)

this way – "Happy is he who is scared of Him who it is fitting to be scared of."

The only fear that is necessary in life is the fear of the Lord. The Hebrew word used for fear in such instances has the sense of having someone watching. Both when we do righteous and unrighteous acts someone is watching. We find great consolation to know, that in good times and in bad times, the guardian of our soul stands watch over us.

Scripture declares that the fear of the Lord is the beginning of wisdom[16]. Having God, our wisdom, enables us to face fear with courage. Wisdom's beauty lies not in the making of right decisions. Its beauty is shown in the resolve to trust God completely. Trusting Him without reservation and acting willingly as He guides and leads whatever the cost may be. Fear is simply a convenient excuse for not fully trusting God.

Earlier in this chapter was the story of a boy who, with all the courage he could muster, entered a dark scary place. Was he able to conquer his fear? Did he get the chance to reach his final destination? Were the goals he meant to achieve fulfilled?

The story goes that he did.

It was just one of the many fears he would face as he stepped into his future. He had to face each one with courage. One thing he found out though, is he didn't have to do it alone. There was a presence, though not visible to his naked eyes, which abided with him on each and every occasion wherein he faced fear. You probably guessed by this time whose presence I am talking about.

---

[16] Job 28:28, Psalm 111:10, Proverbs 9:10

STRENGTH OF HEART

Before I end this chapter, permit me tell you of another story about darkness and the abiding presence.

Here it is:

It was dark when we arrived at this seemingly humble looking edifice. Just a single level as it appeared from our vantage point – the tour bus. Earlier in the morning, on the same bus, we logged in a total of more than 5 hours travel from an international border crossing (river beneath) to this place with one stop over at a mountain peak to view the expanse of a great valley, a calm sea – and from afar the hills of an ancient city.

As I got off the bus I quickly felt the cold drift (probably 10°C) as it softly blew across my body. Quickly I dug through my backpack to fetch my jacket. Such a contrast it was, to the hot weather earlier at the border crossing.

Everywhere I looked, all around me was pitch-black save for everything within the building's outline that was visible to us. I started to get the impression that this was a solitary hotel in the middle of nowhere. Yet I had to confirm with more evidence.

We entered a very nice reception area which was another contrast to the plain looking façade. When we had been handed our room keys and entered the lifts, I eventually figured out that the hotel was built on a cliff's precipice which might mean our rooms could be facing the other side.

The ride on the lifts took us down to our room levels. My wife Gem and I entered our room and immediately as I saw the window curtains I got so excited to see the view behind. As I drew open the curtain in full my suspicion was validated - all my eye could catch were the set of lights that gave luminance to the hotel's open spaces. Beyond the hotel's perimeter was total darkness. No majestic scene to behold.

Sometimes, life is like looking through that hotel room's window at night – nothing visible in the distant space – all but incomprehensible vastness. Beyond the hotel borders stretches out total darkness. It lends us a picture of the fear that prompts and swallows us into oblivion and nothingness. There is no future, there is no tomorrow, there is no moving forward. The only exploit taken is stupor. If only we could recognize the Presence that is all along abiding with us - a very present help in time of need, therefore I will not fear[17], a comforter, a friend, a Paraclete.

Since there was nothing in the darkness to apprehend, I closed the curtains shut, got on with our luggage and prepared items for the following day. Later after we settled in our room, we had a sumptuous dinner and soon afterwards a generous conversation with our friends at the hotel balcony. We went back to our room before the evening got deeper. After a prayer, I kissed Gem good night and slept well all throughout till morning.

I woke up the following day to the sharp rays of light that slipped through the cracks at the curtain ends. A feeling of excitement came over me.

I rushed to draw the curtain once more and to my eager amazement I beheld a grand and splendid sight! I woke up my wife Gem and grabbed my camera, captured a thousand photos and just marveled at the beauty of creation. Surely a mere mortal, like me, can't help but conclude and proclaim with utter confidence – "There must be a divine hand that did these all." One wouldn't be deprived of the elation brought about by the transcendent after facing such splendor. The only response apt for that moment was humility and worship.

---

[17] Psalm 46

STRENGTH OF HEART

As I reflected on that experience I settled in my heart that I can trust Jesus even in the midst of life's darkness. I can face my fear head on, knowing He is with me.

My troubled heart will rest in God alone. A new day is coming and early in the morning will I **draw the curtain once more**.

As the years pass by I find that life does not get easier – at least in my own experience. It doesn't get easier but for certain, it does get sweeter and sweeter. The challenges are much greater, so are the victories that come after the battle. Day by day I bow in humility at the amazing grace given to me. Clearly God's love is unfailing and so creative in its expression.

This is my journey as I march at the fair point of midlife. I have learned to take a stance, expecting a bigger storm approaching but with the assurance that God is the strength of my heart[18].

There are many fears in the past that I have conquered but surely more will come my way – new circumstances, characters, events and experiences I would encounter for the first time.

Will I ever be fearless? Will I ever be without fear?

I know my hands could grow weak and my knees feeble but God commands me to be strong and of good courage.

I know I may fall, get hurt and be wounded, but through His Word I will be reminded that I can stand again.

---

[18] Psalm 73

I know I may run away and hide but at His call I will turn back and stand my ground.

I know my heart and my flesh may fail, but God is the strength of my heart.

I know I will be afraid again yet His presence is with me.

I will face what's before me no matter what the cost may be…*without fear*.

Left to right: Noel, Noel's wife Gemma, daughter Jennifer, and son Jonathan,

EMMANUEL "NOEL" BORBON

Emmanuel Borbon is associate pastor of West Sydney Community Church. Prior to this he served in the same capacity at the Love of Jesus Christian Ministries where he was ordained to the ministry.

He is bi-vocational, and having completed a degree in engineering, has been working in Information Technology for around 28 years.

He lives with his family in Sydney, Australia. Originally from the Philippines, it is there he first served in leadership roles at the Power of God Fellowship. He and wife Gemma are blessed with two grown children –Jonathan and Jennifer.

CHAPTER 3

SHE LOOKS TO THE FUTURE AND SMILES!

By Leslie Bower

"The generous soul will be made rich, and he who waters will also be watered himself."

Proverbs 11:25

"Never give in. Never, never, never, never--in nothing, great or small, large or petty--never give in, except to convictions of honor and good sense. Never yield to force. Never yield to the apparently overwhelming might of the enemy."

~Winston Churchill

I am excited to share some strategies that the Holy Spirit has trained me in, to overcome **fear** and **discouragement**. I have repeatedly tapped into Him in order to find His way through circumstances that were not turning out as I expected.

I would like to give you strategies that put you in a leaning forward position, rather than being stuck and **fearful** that you might fail.

Remember God is on the move and when I leave behind my unmet expectations, I cross over that divide into what is possible through Christ!

To get there, I must **first** realize where I am. We can ask ourselves the following questions to discern this:

Do I see the same thing occurring and not getting different results?

How do I react to unmet expectations – self-pity, depression, or anger?

All of these are dead ends. Aha! I recognize it!!

Secondly, I must look upward.

God reaches down through my "mess" and offers His arm. If I choose to take hold, I crossover to the other side of possibility. I have surrendered the past in order to face the future!

In Jeremiah 29:11 God promises:
"For I know the plans I have for you," declares the Lord, "plans to prosper you and not to harm you, plans to give you a hope and a future."

Let's play this out together…

Focusing on unmet expectations:	If I choose to yield my expectations:
Leads to discouragement	I find peace
Loss of motivation	Exploration, reaching out

SHE LOOKS TO THE FUTURE AND SMILES!

Angry, looking to blame, stuck	Increased possibility
Loss of creativity	Ability to hear the Lord
Isolation, burnout	Solutions not seen before begin to emerge

As Covid 19 began to spread through Seattle in January 2020, my curiosity quickly turned to dismay. I didn't expect to see it cover the whole USA, let alone blanket the world.

At the same time, I was working through treatment for stage 4 lung cancer. I had been diagnosed with it when I got back from a profoundly enjoyable trip to England and Europe with my dear friend Jakki – who passed away a few months before I wrote this book.

On my return home, I knew I needed to see my doctor. After struggling up some steep hills on the last three days of our trip, I was preparing for what I thought would be an issue with my heart.

Instead, my doctor said that the chest x-ray showed a tumor which he suspected was lung cancer. I needed to be seen as soon as possible by the specialist. He prayed for me and encouraged me to stay near the emergency room as it looked like my oxygen levels could be compromised.

I was in complete shock! But while waiting at my son's home, my three boys gathered around me and prayed. Even though a sense of unreality settled around me, I was profoundly grateful that the Lord held off the symptoms of the tumor and collapsed lung until I got back from my trip.

Soon there was a plan to help me go forward with treating the lung cancer.

The Lord was very near to me as I walked through those days. I even had several people who had dreams or visions to share with me.

It became less surreal and more in this time-space world. I am so grateful for the encouragement I received. I will share some of them with you.

My 65th birthday was soon after I was diagnosed in September of 2018. I had a picture of a dusty birthday bag with dirty rags used in place of tissue paper. The rags smelled like diesel and I didn't want to touch them.

However, I sensed the Holy Spirit's urging. I lifted out the rags and peered into the dirty bag, and saw something gleaming. It was a large, multi-colored gem! Underneath all those rags was a treasure. God was giving me an experience to strengthen and establish me against all odds. He was promising to take me forward and reassuring me that I would be ok.

He came to me several times over the next few weeks while I learned that the lung cancer had metastasized to my brain, and my liver.

At one point, I heard Him say, I am the Maker of your frame. I am your Master, not cancer. For each organ afflicted, He said, I am the Maker of your lungs, not cancer; I am the Maker of your brain, not cancer, etc. It was a profound time.

I had been citing: He is the Author and Finisher of my faith. I had held onto Him. He answered me with assurance from Psalm 139, especially verses 15 & 16: *"My frame was not hidden from Thee, when I was made in secret, and skillfully wrought in the depths of the earth. And in Thy Book they were all written, the days that were ordained for me when as yet there were one of them."*

That was a part of the faithfulness of my Lord to me!

So, I returned to a truth that He had shown me. Because I had been able (by His grace) to trust Him with this latest challenge of discovering cancer in my body, I could look to the future, hold onto His leg, and let Him sail the ship through the stormy seas safely.

I am most assured that I will accomplish every day on this earth that the Lord has planned for me!

The following December, my dear granddaughter, Colette, suffered a brain aneurysm due to a rare condition called Arteriovenous Malformation. After experiencing a headache, she fainted. Unconscious, she was rushed to the hospital via ambulance, she stopped breathing along the way and had to be intubated.

Meeting her parents at the hospital, I was taken aback.

Yet in the middle of our shock, I suddenly had a vision of Colette and she was deep in Father God's heart, *without* pain. She was skipping in her favorite prairie dress with her cowboy boots on. I told her mother, "I trust the Lord. If she has an assignment and she says 'Yes', and the Father sends her back, I will be here on her team."

Accompanied by her mom, she was airlifted to Harborview Hospital in Seattle while her dad followed close behind. They didn't know at the time if she would survive. We all prayed for her and spread the word, resulting in a chorus of prayers.

This was so traumatic for Colette and the whole family. After a couple months at Harbourview Medical Center, she was transferred to Seattle Children's Hospital. There was some talk of her future. Her parents wanted to take her home. The Neurosurgeons were concerned that she would have limited ability to improve.

About the time the possibility of going home was put on the calendar, she gave a half smile! She woke up!

This event caused us all to rejoice! Colette's waking up came very slowly…the other half of her smile took several weeks to appear. Her eyes started to follow objects or people as they went by her bed. It delayed her home going because she was transferred to another part of the hospital where the clinicians explored what she may be able to do. This was extremely trying and her progress was slow. It delayed the family's desire of being together again.

I was concurrently being treated with chemotherapy. We stayed united in prayer and on our devices. We still have that unity of the Spirit as we go forward.

As Covid 19 entered the picture, I was used to being flexible. It seemed like a much smaller disruption than the previous issues had. It was less up front and in my face like my family and my health.

However, as it unfolded and the ramifications became more clear, I realized the effects would change our history forever. Businesses were shut down, except what were considered essential ones. Churches and schools were closed. Sports in schools was closed. There seemed no way to protect from the spread of the virus.

Soon we were mandated to stay in our homes. When going out, we were mandated to use a mask to cover our faces and stay 6 feet apart.

SHE LOOKS TO THE FUTURE AND SMILES!

What could I do? It certainly wasn't like I expected.

Then I remembered that God *had* trained me many years ago. When I don't know what to do or how to do it, I can cry out to Him.

He had already sent me His precious Holy Spirit to guide me. And though I might not understand at the time, I can follow! If He closes one way, I surrender. Then I start looking for another way.

I have my guardrails – the Word of God. Jesus said the Holy Spirit will lead me into all truth: *John 16:13 "But when He, the Spirit of truth, comes, He will guide you into all the truth."*

I asked the Lord continually and I kept listening. He reminded me of what I could do. I recalled how Holy Spirit had guided me before. I was secure in my identity in Jesus.

Gradually, through the years of trusting Him, I have put off fears.

The Deepest Trial in my Lifetime

My hardest fears were surrounding the loss of my husband. I was forty-four when he passed on to be with the Lord. We had been very close and I was torn apart by his leaving.

That was the deepest trial in my lifetime. I clung to the Lord. He had passed away at forty five from a Grand Mal Seizure. I found him in the orchard. He liked to go to this certain place where he could see Mt. Adams. He was an early riser and when he didn't come back in, I went looking for him, and I found him there.

When the Sheriff came to get his body, they asked to do an autopsy. I was very interested to know what he had died from. The coroner contacted me to say that he had died of a Grand Mal seizure. This was so sudden and unexpected.

Friends and relatives filled the church and I was greatly comforted by their support.

Two weeks after his funeral, I had a visit from the sheriff's office. An investigator came to see where he had expired. I was puzzled, as photos had already been taken; there had been an investigation at the time of death.

A few days later it came out that there was a report from the state lab that had checked my husband's blood from a sample sent in by the coroner. It detected Strychnine Poison in the blood sample! I didn't know what to do with this information.

I was blown to and fro.

The coroner said that the body was **not** evidencing the poison But the investigator began to accuse me of covering up murder or suicide.

I again had the surreal feeling to reality. I was called by Holy Spirit to look to Him. Imagine the pain of losing my husband, on top of being unable to explain or understand the circumstances, and then now this accusation?!

The Lord told me out loud, "Don't speculate." I realized that the whole thing must be put into my Lord's hands, I needed to follow the instructions from Him:

"Rejoice in the Lord always, again I say rejoice! Let your forbearing spirit be made known to all men. The Lord is near. Be anxious for nothing but in everything with prayer and supplication with

thanksgiving, let your requests be made known to God. And the peace of God which surpasses all comprehension, shall guard hearts and your minds in Christ Jesus. Finally brethren, whatever is true, whatever is honorable, whatever is right, whatever is pure, whatever is lovely, whatever is of good repute, if there is any excellence and anything worthy of praise, let your mind dwell on these things. The things you have learned and received, and heard and seen, practice these things. And the God of peace will be with you." Philippians 4:4-9

I treated these as instructions. I began to implement them. I thanked the Lord out loud for His faithful leading as I did this. I turned away from the darkness which sought to entangle me and instead, turned towards the Holy Spirit, who patiently waited for me.

A friend called and told me it wasn't my responsibility to figure this out. The Lord had it figured it out and it was in His hands.

I had so much prayer support. I kept working out my salvation, so to speak, as the days moved forward. I was aware that there was something at stake.

I kept praying for His kingdom to come, His will to be done, surrendering to Him and being flexible. I was surprised by the kindness of people all around me, willing to support me and my family without having to answer questions that I could not answer for myself. I would have to leave my questions with God and trust Him with the answers.

I went on with living out His purpose on this earth.

Serendipitously, this led me into real estate investing. After reading *Rich Dad Poor Dad by Robert Kiyosaki*, the Holy Spirit kept me looking at a piece of property that was on my route when I used to walk to church.

One day, I was surprised to see a for sale sign on that property, so I bought it! My 3 sons built a home on it, and after several years, they each profited from it.

Even though I was a beginner, the Holy Spirit additionally blessed me with 6 rentals! Can you see how the Lord has tremendously helped me to move from potentially being fearful of the future, to becoming **fearless**, no matter what the situation or circumstance?

It was important to my husband and me to be a part of helping each son to purchase his first home. Each one of my sons has either built or purchased a home. God is good and has fulfilled my heart's desire.

In the wake of the national economic crisis, a local bank continued working with me although other banks were put in jeopardy. I now own 3 of the 6 rentals outright, including my own home! Equity has increased on each house, and I am amazed at how the Lord has prospered me and I have an inheritance for my children.

Each story includes the Lord reaching out to me and pulling me out of the unmet expectations. Each time, I'm aware of His comfort and care for me. Then He helps me position. Releasing all fear, I begin to go forward to what is possible in the Lord Jesus.

The Holy Spirit reminded me of another **key** that sometimes goes with disappointed expectations.

I want to emphasize this point to you. I found that in cases wherein I am offended, this is an indication that could be a coldness in my heart or a fear that directs my action – which I must put before the Lord. I go before Him and ask Him to show me. I can then ask forgiveness for that circumstance, for myself or another person.

And whenever you stand praying, forgive, if you have anything against anyone, so your Father who is in heaven may forgive you your trespasses. Mark 11:25

Without my heart being open to His revealing and cleansing blood applied to what He reveals, I will be walled up, unable to receive His intervention.

For example, I needed to open my heart to the investigator in his accusations. I forgave him and then I was free from what he was spreading. Yes, I still took action, as was appropriate, but I didn't allow anger or hurt to rule over me. I was able to go *forward* **without fear**.

The need for me to switch from my expectations to the appearance of new possibilities is *seldom* smooth sailing. It is in the midst of peace and joy as I go along being led by Him.

My life has been full of His love and encouragement; of other like-minded family and extending to other Believers. I'm so grateful for all the life He has planned for me to discover!

Through many toils and snares I have already come, 'twas Christ that brought me safe thus far and Christ will lead me home! (adapted from former English navy seaman, poet and clergyman John Newton's song – "Amazing Grace")

L→R Liliana, Beckett, William, Ellis, Trenton (holding Ellis), Cassius (in front of Trenton), Beth, Skyler, Addison, Suzanne, Ethan, Jared, Janelle

L→R Seated and standing: Colette (in wheelchair), Leslie, Ella, Jack, Lauren

LESLIE BOWER

Leslie is currently a Grandma of 11 children – each one of whom she treasures! She prays for her family and friends, America the Beautiful, and the World. She wants to influence others to look to Jesus as Lord and Savior and to glorify Him. She has been surrendering to the Lord since she was 16 years old. He has proven His faithfulness over and over.

Leslie was a pastor's wife for 10 years. She was encouraged and supported by her husband, her family and a great church family.

She is the best selling author of "Guard Against Burnout – 7 Proven Keys to Help You Thrive in the Dental Field." She is accomplished in the field of dentistry as a Registered Dental Hygienist for 45 years while being supported by a great team.

Connect with Leslie Bower via email: ldbower12310@yahoo.com

CHAPTER 4
NIL DESPERANDUM!
COVID19, Lockdown and the Aftermath
By Kenneth Jao

The effects of the lockdown were devastating, eroding personal and business confidence. The simplicity of that statement belies the grave enormity of its impact.

In my efforts to craft clear guidelines for my business direction, amidst the worsening health and business climate, I recalled the effects of recent yet historic financial downturns: the **1997** Asian Financial Crisis and the **2008** Financial Meltdown. Understanding both events aided me in handling the present pandemic. However, this was not as easy, due to the specter of the health system's collapse, should things take a turn for the worst.

I want to describe to you what my company and I faced in the midst of the crisis, from every angle, especially its health and safety impact, as well as the effects on business and the economy.

To be able to describe and evaluate the effects, one should be able to describe the pre-pandemic situation, developments during the pandemic, and what everyone will be facing in the new normal.

Pre-Lockdown (Two Weeks Before March 12, 2020)

Manila was placed under lockdown effective March 12, 2020.

Prior to lockdown, everything seemed to be going well. Plans were afoot to obtain new contracts and fresh work. Business was humming along on a nice steady clip. My company was in negotiations with several other companies and we were already in the process of perfecting contract documents with important clients.

One of our projects even had a ground breaking, signifying the start of the project. We were working with several big name developers, as well as government clients, in order to initialize new projects. We also gained approval for additional working capital lines with one of our lenders, signifying confidence in our situation. Moreover, our development loan was approved and implementation was well underway. In all, everything was going well at the start of 2020 and couldn't have been better.

Then, quite ominously, rumors started circulating about a possible lockdown amongst the senior government officials with whom I was acquainted.

As I was very aware of the current situation in China and the rest of the world, I made sure I paid heed to what was being discussed in the corridors of power.

Two weeks before the lockdown, I promptly directed my senior personnel, to draft lockdown protocols. I assumed that the need for such would ensure the safety of everyone and preserve whatever resources we needed to endure the lockdown.

Candidly, I estimated a 45 to 60-day lockdown, hence, we felt prepared for that. But, at the back of everyone's mind, was that remote possibility of not having done enough. However, I stuck to my guns and continued pressing my people for lockdown and re-start protocols.

I had my personnel talking with everyone at our sites, about what to do, from the wage situation to the work rotations, and, the relief goods to be sent should the lockdown cause severe disruptions. We also discussed with suppliers for the need to suspend scheduled deliveries and re-arrange schedules on almost everything. My personnel were perplexed, but, they followed what I asked them to do. I was branded in the industry as a "heretic," based on my directions. But still, we moved ahead. That action likely saved us a lot of grief in handling on-site personnel, as most were given salaries and ordered to stay home, upon the lockdown announcement. My work sites each had a skeletal workforce, guarding and manning the jobsites and the inventories. It was a prudent action to take at that time, although, now I wonder if more drastic measures should have been undertaken.

Looking back, when the lockdown was extended, the government provided no clear directions or guidelines. This took me aback and fostered greater worry.

We refrained from using the word "lockdown" in all our inter-company memos and instructions, we instead used the word "quarantine". We were all optimistic about the situation. I was continuously optimistic and kept thinking to myself that this would be just a "pause" and everything would be alright.

Sadly, we were unprepared for the situation that slowly unfolded.

The Quarantine period: ECQ, MECQ, GSCQ (March 15 to present)

During times of war and crisis, I know that communications and logistics are of paramount importance.

The situation we were faced with was both a war and a crisis, hence the importance of communicating and providing direction and guidance to everyone. The ability to convey and carry out assistance thru logistics was also a pressing concern.

Social Atmosphere

Everyone was perplexed by the severity of the situation. As the days went by, information steadily provided us with the reality of the situation. Literature on the effects of the disease, symptoms, and scenarios slowly built up the face of the threat. Further, the situation from other countries facing Covid-19 came in steadily, through news and social media. The global effects were clear and distressing.

The news of death rates slowly rising and climbing up to numbers unheard of except during times of war - seemed absurd at first, but soon became normal news.

Everyone I knew, who was in lockdown, initially felt it was a simple "holiday vacation" of sorts. All movement was restricted. Simple transactions were difficult to pursue. Government directions and initiatives were unclear. It was to me a nightmare slowly coming into reality. I told myself, whatever will come next, after the lockdown, will be much more difficult than the lockdown itself.

The seemingly annoying, and at times mind-numbing, social media became the de facto source of information for the majority. From mindless banter to informative commentaries and suggestions: one had to carefully sift through the cacophony of voices to find the right information on health and safety.

Business Atmosphere

Optimism was the order of the day during the early period of the quarantine. The business atmosphere during those times showed signs of optimism from every sector and industry that I knew of.

But the number of infected people slowly rose, from below a hundred a day to the now much more mind-boggling a thousand a day average. This eroded everyone's confidence, much more so, as the days went by and the increasing numbers shot up.

Thanfully, there was some government action. The Bayanihan Act 1 (the "BA1") was a welcome legislation. The "…to Heal as One Act," the BA1, or also called Republic Act No. 11469, was an emergency response implementing important measures to allay public fears of the pandemic.

It authorized the President to implement measures for the effective detection of the virus among the populace; prompt testing by health facilities of patients; protection and access to transportation in favor of our frontline health workers; maintenance of availability and pricing of essential and basic commodities; and provision of relief goods to vulnerable sectors of society, among others.

It quickly dawned on everyone that, without the BA1, the bills would pile up, bank creditors would be knocking on everyone's door, with no help in sight for everyone in business. Also business closures, unemployment, and all the other negative effects of the pandemic would escalate.

To make matters worse, the constant fear of getting infected and the possibility of dying alone in the hospital was becoming a reality.

Social media rapidly transformed into the driving force for commerce, what was once in the background of the social fabric entrenched itself front and center in the economic order of things. The seeming novelty of e-commerce became a necessity for everyone. The novelty had passed and social media is now a central pattern of the new normal.

It is also during these times that I reached out to other businessmen I know. It became clear that no one was spared from worrying about the situation. They were as worried as me about the bills piling, no revenues coming in, bank interests and loans coming due, projects on hold, everything on hold, on pause, much like the sword of Damocles hanging above everyone's head ready to bring down dreadful demise with the snap of a string.

In summary, what was an optimistic atmosphere quickly became a quicksand of pessimism. Although BA1 helped, a large portion was left unclear; hence, a much more direct and clear approach was needed, . Seemingly, all hope of recovery had vanished without any means of assistance from the government.

Only the signing of the Bayanihan Act 2 (BA2) on the second reading gave hope for government assistance and direction on what was needed but everything was still opaque on thealth and safety issues. Without government-mandated assistance, recovery would be painful and difficult with most businesses under threat of closure.

Today and the rest of the Pandemic Years

I will summarize what I feel today and perhaps for the next couple of months or years:

- loss of confidence in doing business safely and profitably;
- loss of confidence in doing business due to the present business atmosphere;
- fear for the health and safety of my personnel, my family and myself;
- loss of confidence in what the government actions; and
- fear of the rise in criminal activities due to loss of income for the majority.

Despite that dreadful assessment, there is however, a silver lining to it all and as a businessman, I must and should be able to navigate these shoals despite the situation.

I believe that opportunities are present in this crisis.

I am a Filipino of Chinese descent, and it was taught to us that in crisis, there abounds opportunity; much like the Chinese character for crisis, it is composed of the word danger and opportunity or a change point.

Those who will be able to navigate and be creative thinkers will not only survive, but will thrive. Careful and meticulous planning is greatly needed. In this, the government must give incentives for the business sector in the form of tax breaks.

The government must encourage business activity that works within the framework of the new normal which includes new ways of thinking and new ways of doing business.

There must be some order in the measures and guidelines being mandated by the government and there must be clear directions given on how things need to be done. The infrastructure to ensure acceptance and access to the vaccine, by all, must be set in place.

There is a general lack of confidence in going out to work, particularly because of the government's lack of guidance and direction. This may also be due to the lack of moral authority of some government officials. News of rampant corruption in handling the budget for the pandemic response abounds.

People are looking forward to new laws that will enact the government's support to the business sector providing definitive direction and assistance.

I fear that the best option for most businessmen will be a temporary closure until everything returns to a semblance of normalcy. This is despite the opportunities which I see are in place. As a business owner, I can act for my business, but the growing burden of operating under a cloud of uncertainty is not for the faint hearted. It is therefore imperative that government create clear directions, concrete guidance, and a solid action plan coupled with broad assistance for business to rebound and flourish.

The migration to e-commerce is a bright spot but not all businesses are able to operate under the e-commerce platform, particularly the construction industry where physical presence and physical capacity is a must.

The COVID19 has long-term effects whose aftermath is not yet in sight, the full economic impact and devastation will likely be felt in the last quarter of this year (2021). I sincerely hope that the government will be able to pull itself together in assisting Filipinos and providing decisive leadership.

However, despite these sentiments of doom and gloom, I am determined to meet the challenges of doing business in the "new normal" head on. All I need is time and some assistance to enable my plans, as I am confident that all these things will come to pass.

I am in the construction and development business and I am fully aware that the construction industry will provide the much needed push for all the other industries. Hence, there is a need to be able to survive the present situation and prepare for the coming economic resurgence. Somehow, that provides me with relief and a sense of optimism on my part.

Right now, I wonder how we will look back at all these things years from now.

Years ago, as a young man, my father sent me alone on an errand to mainland China. I was to look for his friend. Mind you, this was in the 1990s during the infancy of the internet, without all the gadgets, connectivity, online maps and other things we enjoy today.

I took a train all the way to Ulan Bator. The money I had was only enough for food and passage. I had to fend for myself and find resourceful ways and means. I had to travel to Wenzhou, Dalian, Chong Qing, Sze Chuan, Fu Zhou, among others.

I ventured to the unknown, bravely, because the directions were clear: who to see, where to go, and what to do, even if the mission was rife with unknowns.

Of course, I made it. I believe I am on the same journey now as I was back then.

> *"I learned that courage is not the absence of fear, but the triumph over it."*
>
> ~Nelson Mandela

KENNETH JAO

Kenneth Jao was born in the Philippines and studied at the best university the country could offer.

He set up his own business and dedicated himself to the ideals of being able to share the fruits of wealth and prosperity with everyone.

He looks forward to enjoying the joys of travel with his wife soon.

CHAPTER 5
IT ALL BEGAN
By Maria Theresa Trono-Legiralde

Naively Fearless

I have two elder brothers who made me think and act boyish. I never liked wearing girlie clothes and would always prefer sporting a ponytail.

I remember my eldest brother teaching me how to pull a punch! This got me interested in enrolling in Karate class when I was in University.

He would also ask me for a massage after a tiring day from his vanguard training at U.P. (the University of the Philippines). My father would comment that I had strong hands as I would sometimes give my parents a massage as I did with my eldest brother.

I learned to carry heavy stuff which most girls my age would not want to do. When I was in elementary, I already had calloused my hands as I regularly carried basketfuls of food bought from the market.

My uncle Inciong (my father's cousin) who was a carpenter, made one pool table. I watched them play until I got interested and he taught me the basics. He even taught me how to handle carpentry tools.

I always thought to myself: I want to be physically strong and able to do what boys my age can do.

How I loved the TV series "Bionic Woman" and I always wanted to be the person who could stand up and protect herself when things got rough. I needed to be **fearless** when facing difficult situations and not be the limp girl who cannot even pull a punch when needed. I can remember situations where, thinking back today, I was naively **fearless**.

Or so I thought I was fearless.

Bike Ride To The Market

It was summertime and I was wearing shorts and a t-shirt, my hair tied into a ponytail. My bike screeched as I pressed on the brakes to a sudden stop. I heard street boys on the other side of the road, wolf whistling when I passed. One of them was even trying to introduce himself while the rest were laughing. I told myself, I will not let this pass. I hated it when men were rude to women. I stared at them with a deathly stare and shouted, *"If you don't have anything to do decent, go home to your mom and have your mouth washed with laundry soap."* They scoffed at me even more and I continued to stare straight at them while they laughed at me. As it was a busy street, jeepneys and tricycles passed and blocked my sight.

I then decided to bike back home before things got ugly.

The Garden Raiders

When I was in elementary, I loved home economics. Part of the subject matter was gardening, and we got to bring home our produce. My group mates were equally good with the soil, and had green thumbs as they say.

My secret: I collected dried carabao (water buffalo) dung from the nearby field and would pound it so it could mix easily with the garden soil. It was almost a week prior to harvest. We expected a good harvest as our *"pechay"* (cabbages) were all so healthy, thanks to the carabaos.

My group mates went ahead as I prepared something before heading to the garden. As I approached them, one of the girls ran towards me and was whispering something to my ear. I could not understand at first as she was breathing heavily and sounded scared. I told her to calm down and speak slowly.

She hastily warned me not to go near the garden as there was a group of outsiders whom they had caught stealing our "pechay" that we were supposed to harvest that day.

Blood rushed to my head, I got boiling mad and rushed to the site. I **fearlessly** shouted at the "outsiders", *"Who do you think you are? I could call the school securities to arrest you for trespassing. You better leave our "pechay" and get out of here!!"*

During the altercation, another group mate was trying to pull me aside and was whispering to let it go as one of the outsiders had a handheld knife. This made me even more aggressive and I kept shouting at them to get out of the property or else! Luckily, they did, but with our "pechay".

Otherwise, I would have gotten us into trouble.

Hitchhikers

The typhoon was packing strong winds and the rain was pouring. Storm signals were raised that afternoon and we were sent home.

Our umbrellas were useless, but we had our raincoats on. My sister, Jo and I were able to ride the bus from U.P. High (the University of the Philippines has its own high school) to EDSA (E. De Los Santos Avenue – the main freeway that linked the university to several surrounding cities).

But as we waited at the bus stop, I noticed that there was no traffic along EDSA and there were less motorists and public transports plying the streets (probably due to the floods).

I wondered if we could even get home from Quezon City to Caloocan City as there seemed to be no public transport in sight…and if there was, it was jam-packed full. And even if we could get a taxi from Quezon Avenue, we did not have enough money at the time.

So, we waited, and waited.

We were hungry and cold, as it got darker by the minute. I told myself I must make a decision immediately – because I wouldn't want us getting stuck there without shelter, no food and with the storm raging. So I told Jo, we had three options: wait for a bus, walk home, or hitchhike.

I told my sister that if we decided to hitchhike, we would try to spot an elderly driver and we needed to sit at the back seat together. I was praying hard but at the same time asking myself if this was the right option under the circumstances.

I, being the older sibling, needed to make the decision. Then, we agreed to hitchhike home. I was **afraid** and so was my sister. We did the hitchhiker's sign at motorists passing by.

One sedan stopped, he had no one with him and he asked where we were heading. I said "Monumento Caloocan City, Mister". He then invited us to hop in as he said he was going that direction.

As planned, my sister and I sat at the back and as far as I can remember I was holding a pen, just in case. We were both quiet during the ride. But I was praying for safety. And I know my sister did likewise. And thank God, this kindhearted man dropped us at Monumento, Caloocan.

I do not ever remember telling my parents that we did hitchhike. I was so thankful to God, we got home safe.

But I thought to myself, I wouldn't be able to forgive myself if something bad had happened to my sister.

Visiting Aunty Rosario

After more than a year of employment as a research aide, my father encouraged me to take up a Master's Degree at U.P. in the Visayas, Iloilo. He advised that his roots were in Leon, Iloilo. He reminded me that my Aunty Rosario, who took care of me when I was a toddler, lived there.

It was a hard decision to make, but I understood the wisdom of my father.

Halfway during my academics at UPV (University of the Philippines – Visayas branch), I finally decided to visit my Aunty.

I asked my classmates where I needed to ride to reach Leon. They asked if my Auntie knew that I was in Iloilo. I said no, I do not have a way to advise them. Besides, I do not even know their address in Leon. They gave me directions but were worried that I was leaving an hour before dusk and had no clue of my Aunt's address.

The jeepney ride was bumpy but I was able to get an occasional nap.

I requested the driver to drop me off at the town market. As I walked towards the marketplace, I noticed the stalls were closed and a few people were going about their closing chores. I asked around for Aunt Rosario.

As the town was small, everyone practically knew who lives around each corner. At the mention of my Aunt's name, a lady gladly led me to her stall. I was lucky enough to catch her as she was on her way home. When I introduced myself, I asked for her hands of blessing (_"mano"_ – a gesture of respect for the elderly) as she expressed her delight to seeing me again and hugged me as if I was still a small chubby girl. *"Oh my, Maritess, you are all so grown up. You were so small when I left you"*. We gleefully chatted in the tricycle going home. However, she reprimanded me, saying it was a dangerous thing for me to have travelled alone, not speaking good Ilonggo and at worst, it was getting dark. I told her I wanted to visit her. Besides, I was not **afraid** to travel alone. I just need to ask for direction and people are always kind to help a stranger.

She warned about NPA's but the most dangerous are _"mangkukulams"_ (witches) or _"nuno sa punso"_ - dwarf-like nature spirit (anito), who might get interested in me, a stranger. She said witches are known in their place as targeting new faces especially girls. I was laughing at her stories about folklore and told her not to worry as I do not believe in them. And, to try to convince me, she even warned me to close the bedroom windows made of Capiz as it was getting dark. She said there is a *"tikbalang"* - half man-half horse living in the big tree just outside the bedroom window who might get interested and kidnap me. I told her I prefer my windows open when I sleep as I want to feel the cool night breeze. But I did pray for protection (just in case) and I slept soundly that night.

The next day after hearty lunch, my Aunt requested a relative to accompany me to the city as I got back to my boarding house. During the ride back to the city, I was thinking at the back of my mind: Oh goodness!! What if Auntie Rosario was right?!!

Aha! .... that scared me a bit, I guess.

Hope Deferred and Longing Fulfilled

Years of Grind

Fast forward, after graduating from my master's studies, I found myself loving the job I had with the Technology & Livelihood Resource Centre (TLRC) as a technical consultant, project appraiser/evaluator, and in my private capacity as a technical trainer for selected aquaculture training courses.

However, I saw the slow-paced progress of my career in government service. I thought to myself, "My career may not be able to keep up with the financial demands of sending our children to good education. This made me **fearful** for my children's future.

During that time, one of the team leaders in our department migrated to New Zealand. After years in NZ, he visited us, his former colleagues, and encouraged me to try applying for migration, as my educational and work background had a place in their Fisheries / Aquaculture industry.

I was **afraid** at first as this would mean charting foreign territory and re-establishing ourselves. I shelved the idea for quite some time, but the thought of migrating came back whenever I saw our debts increasing each year just to send the children to school.

When my eldest daughter was already in high school, I got the courage to convince my husband to try applying and if God opened the door, then we would take the next steps.

However, during that same period, TLRC offered an early retirement plan. I prayed that I needed to get a job first before I even decided to take the retirement offer.

I landed a job with a well known foundation, as a project development consultant to a managing director of the new institute, and later for another role.

It was a five year stint, which I thought would propel me to a position that would be rewarding. But somehow, things changed, and I was disheartened to see myself forced into the same workplace culture I had in government service.

This situation pushed us to aggressively pursue the immigration application. When we did, our papers did not progress with the agency we had engaged. More time passed.

IT ALL BEGAN

So, I kept praying. If God wanted me to stay with the Foundation, He had a purpose. And if God opened a new opportunity for me then, it would be time to exit the foundation.

Unfortunately, job applications were turned down one after another. This was not exactly how I wanted things to happen.

My fear of the future was mounting.

A Stranger's Call

It was a tiring ride back home after work. As usual, I took naps when I could.

Suddenly, my phone rang and I noted that the number was not in my directory. I hesitated to pick up the call but decided to accept it.

A male voice asked the question, "Is this Maria Theresa Legiralde?" I replied with a question asking who / what his name was and where he got my mobile number. He quickly explained that he was a client of the same immigration agency and informed me that it was closing due to scam cases being filed against the company. He instructed me to get our passports and papers from the office as it would be closed down in two days' time due to the investigation by the NBI (National Bureau of Investigation).

After the call, I was crying out to God asking what we were to do next, why this was happening, and what were our options. I wept for the remainder of the bus ride, **fearful** of what this might mean for our family.

I discussed this with my husband, who met with this stranger the next day, and they were able to retrieve our papers. We were back to square one.

My husband and I discussed options. We realized that INZ sent the agency a letter asking the agent to submit pertinent papers, including our passports, so they could approve our work-to-residence visas. But since the agency was bombarded with demand letters, it went bankrupt.

Thus, our papers were in "limbo" and the deadline to submit required papers and passports has passed.

I told my husband that we could try a petition letter explaining the circumstances behind the delays. If they reconsidered, we would proceed, if not, then God had other plans.

It was a season of crying out for God's help and favor. *I was fearful of both possibilities: Migrating to New Zealand, or staying where we were.*

Fourth Watch of the Night

I remember I had a hard time sleeping that night due to the warm, humid climate.

At around half past three in the morning, I was awakened, sweating, and had to get up to drink water. I tried to get back to sleep but could not. It was two hours away from my wake-up alarm.

Frustrated, I sat up and took my bible, hoping that I will get tired reading and catch an hour of sleep.

God led me to read Joshua 1:1-9 and as I was reading it, God strongly impressed the phrases *"be strong and courageous"*, which was repeated three times in the passages. As I was reading the verses, I was crying my heart out to God, **fearful**.

Suddenly, I felt God's awesome peace fill my **fearful** heart. It was like a mix of emotions and thoughts, asking God to help me trust Him even though I was drowning in **fear**.

I said *"Lord, "I am so **afraid**; I do not know what to do but I will hold on to these promises and instructions. Help me see what You want me to do and where we are going. You do know my husband has retired, hoping that this migration option would open. Lord, we do not even have enough savings. Our debt is becoming unmanageable each year."*

With tears in my eyes, God led me to read the verses again and again. A particular verse soaked my heart with faith in my God, my good Father.

> *Joshua 1:9 NIV "Have I not commanded you?*
> *Be strong and courageous. Do not be afraid;*
> *do not be discouraged, for the LORD your God*
> *will be with you wherever you go."*

Favor in the Desert

It was another busy day in the office, and I was going through emails. I noticed an email from a commercial bank, offering a multi-purpose loan. If we could offer a collateral, they advised I could use the funds for business or home improvement or any emergency needs.

I discussed this with my husband. We thought of using the funds for the home business I was trying to expand (if our

WTR visas were declined) and/or back up funds in case our WTR (Work to Residence) visas were approved.

Soon enough, the loan was approved and disbursed with our residential lot as collateral.

A few months after we sent off the petition letter to Immigration NZ, we received a reply, requesting submission of pertinent documents for approval of the WTR visa.

Three short weeks after submission, we received our passports with WTR stamps and student visas for our children!

With the events that followed, I was in awe that God had given us favor in the sight of men.

I eventually submitted my resignation from the foundation, but with the request, that should we fail to make it successfully in NZ within a period of nine months, I would be able to return to my position with the foundation.

The CEO and the managing director approved the special request but were saddened by my resignation. They even tried to convince me not to leave the foundation expressing their confidence in me and the importance of my role in the institute.

However, within my **fearful** heart, there was a compelling and reassuring voice, that it was time to move.

I assessed at that time that the remaining funds from the loan would not even be enough for three months. This made me question my decision and so I asked God for provisions.

Two or three weeks prior to our departure, my father asked my husband to accompany a possible buyer to view their property in Quezon City. A week before our departure, the Deed of Sale was finalized and signed, bank payment was processed. To my delight and surprise, my parents gave my husband his commission, enough to help us through! This was the fastest "miracle", that God has done for us. In addition, my parents gave us additional funds to help.

I was awed at God's works and perfect timing. But most of all, awed and humbled knowing how much God loves us.

> *Matthew 6:31-32 ESV "Therefore,*
> *do not be anxious, saying,*
> *'What shall we eat?' or 'What shall we*
> *drink?' or 'What shall we wear?' For the*
> *Gentiles seek after all these things,*
> *and your heavenly Father knows*
> *that you need them all."*

Heart Break

Our departure date was 15 Oct 2010. If I remember correctly, our flight was very early in morning. Feels familiar - fourth watch of the night. Saying goodbye was heart breaking. I told my children to kiss and hug Grandpa and Grandma, their aunties, uncles and cousins. When it was my turn to say goodbye, my father's parting words, *"take care and look after my grandchildren."* My mother was already crying as she hugged me tightly and said *"we love you and will be praying for you all. If you have the chance, do call us. Love you, my daughter"*. I quickly turned around after saying *"I love you Dad and Mom"*, trying not to cry.

The ride to the airport was quiet and felt like a long trip. My sister Jo and her husband Francis, her son Joshua and my brother Romy and my sister in-law Anne were with us. When we arrived at the airport, before getting off the car, my sister Jo hugged me so tightly as she cried saying *"I love you and will miss you dearly"*. Hugs and kisses, the feelings I will never forget.

Fearful, but at the same time I needed to be fearless because I knew God wanted me to trust Him each passing day.

Groundwork in the Desert

A grueling 10-hour flight. For me there was a rush of **fear**, doubt and loneliness. I wanted to run to my "happy place", but I could not. I was crying most of the waking hours during the flight.

We arrived Auckland airport very early in the morning, it was still dark, and we were all so exhausted from the long flight.

My former team leader, whom I now call Tito Demi ("Uncle" Demi), and my colleague from the foundation, Doreen and her husband fetched us. Doreen was kind enough to request her cousin to "adopt us" for a few days while we on our job search, a suitable place and establish our network.

The priority was for us to find a job, any job.

The beauty of springtime did not excite me, as we were solely focused on relentlessly putting our heads together to apply for jobs.

October passed quickly, still no job.

IT ALL BEGAN

November made my heart homesick because Christmas was just like a blink away, and still no job.

December was grueling and discouraging since most companies are on holiday breaks and typically don't hire during this month. Still no job.

We attended two Christian fellowships during these first few months. A Filipino couple (Nel and Jim), in their desire to help, invited us to visit their former church, a multi-cultural church, majority of whom were Pacific Islanders. They said that we needed to meet the Pastor who might be able to help find a suitable job for us.

So that day, we had a brief meeting with the Pastor, and we prayed for God's favor. Before leaving the church premises, Nel grabbed my hands to introduce me to a group of charming ladies outside the church building. We warmly shook hands, and it felt as though I was meeting kindred spirits – warm and hospitable.

As I was introduced to the last lady in the group, she shook my hands, while looking straight into my eyes. She moved me aside and did not let go of my hands. She looked again into my eyes, now holding my two hands together and as she glanced into my open palms and lovingly whispered to me, *"The Lord has placed something very heavy in your hands. But take heart and hold on to God and He will see you through."*

Crown of God's Bounty

The new year 2011 arrived, it seemed bleak for me. We had experienced so many declines and not enough funds. Each job application was like a mirage in the desert, as it was the tail end of the recent recession.

Five months has passed, I had a casual job with McDonald's McCafe. My husband also had casual jobs but not one that would give us our residency visa.

We decided to ask for financial help from my parents as we applied for an extension of our WTR / student visas. Thankfully, the Lord granted this prayer again, and we were given a three-month extension.

Daytime was spent on job hunting and networking. Our evenings were tearful nights of prayer, claiming God's promises.

Our bathroom in the city apartment became my special place where I had my devotions. One evening as I was crying out to God to give us a breakthrough, the Lord in His compassion and mercy led me to read Psalm 65. He impressed in my heart, that He answers with His awesome and righteous deeds – this year is crowned with His bounty.

I suddenly burst out into tears as I felt His loving presence envelop my **fearful** heart.

Psalm 65: 5, 9-11
You answer us with awesome and righteous deeds, God our Savior, …You care for the land and water it; you enrich it abundantly. The streams of God are filled with water to provide the people with grain, for so you have ordained it. You drench its furrows and level its ridges; you soften it with showers and bless its crops. You crown the year with your bounty, and your carts overflow with abundance.

IT ALL BEGAN

Finally, in the third month of our extension, the manager of the sub-contracting firm my husband was working for offered to help and they worked out a job contract for a permanent position that would hopefully satisfy the requirements for a residence visa.

We were all thrilled and profoundly grateful that God granted this prayer!

July came, it was mid-way winter in New Zealand.

I received a call from a potential employer. It was a telephone interview.

I remember that he spoked so fast (and I was still learning to listen to the Kiwi accent), I did my best to answer satisfactorily. But in my heart, I was praying for and relying on God's favor.

At one point, he asked, *"Do you think you can perform well in this role (a customer service position)?"* I promptly responded, *"I would not apply if I do not think I cannot serve the demands of the role"*.

Oh, my – I was taken aback by my own answer and thought to myself, "He might think I am too confident of my myself – perhaps even borderline proud".

The next week came, and to my delight, I was invited for another interview, this time on company premises. Two team leaders interviewed me.

Following the second round of interviews, I received another call for a third interview, this time a panel interview with the CEO, Manager and Team Leader! I was so grateful I reached that level in the interview process, and at the same time, I was prayerful that God would open this door for me.

I arrived 20 minutes early, and was sitting at the reception area, when a gentleman approached me and introduced himself – it was the CEO. He led me to the interview room and the Manager and Team Leader joined us.

During the last week of July, 2011 – I received a call from the manager of the Customer Service Department who offered the job to me!

She requested me to come to the office and sign my first ever permanent full time job contract and submit other documents. I was to report August 1, 2011.

After the job contract signing and a brief tour of the office, my Manager accompanied me as I left the building. When we got to the door, she smiled and revealed her yardstick during my final panel interview,

"I watched you as you sat down calmly, taking off your winter jacket. I smiled when I noticed you folding your jacket neatly and rolling it up to fit it into your second bag which you had on a chair beside you. So, I said to myself, we are making a right decision taking her into this team."

On my way home, I was ecstatic, so grateful, I kept praising God while flashbacks played in my memory. I recalled how God had never failed me, and how He made me face my **fears** by trusting Him every step of the way. Because He had ordained and decreed that He would provide us with "grain", He prepared the groundwork in the desert and crowned the year with His bounty.

Our mirage in the desert turned into a year crowned with God's bounty.

Be Strong and Courageous

When God placed the desire for me to teach a small bible study group, I said, *"Lord, I will not teach anything that I have not personally experienced nor understood. Any topic that you will lead me to share should be from a personal "rhema" you have brought me for very specific situations in life. I need the power of your Holy Spirit to illuminate me and enrich my faith for me to have that total abandonment of trust in myself and full trust in You. To know and love you more each day. That I will be an echoing board, for others to hear You speak to their hearts."*

So, one time, as I was preparing for a bible study, the Lord brought me back to Joshua 1:1-9. I had read these verses many times before.

This time, God gave me a different perspective of being strong and courageous.

Well, first of all, my growing up years made me realize that, in all honesty, I had a **fearful** heart. I may have exhibited a "strong and independent girl" outlook but soon enough I knew what it was like to **fear** "what happens next."

I realized my strength and courage to face life's journey is anchored in my full trust in HIM. My full trust in Him is dependent on my desire to know Him more each day – which nurtures my love for Him.

He made me realize that my strength and courage are anchored in my confidence in who God is in my life.

My deliberate awareness of His active presence in my life will be key to my building a monument of remembrance (stones of memorial) of what, where, how, when, and why of each of

God's miraculous encounters and interventions in my life. That for each **"fearful"** turn, I have a monument of remembrance of what God has done and can do for me.

All for His glory.

He knows that my heart reacts **fearfully** to the "known unknowns and unknown unknowns" in life. But one truth I hold on to: I have a loving Father, the all-powerful God who loves me so much and He will see me through as He holds my hands in this journey.

The One who loves me, leads and commands me to obedience – to be strong in my faith, courageous with the confidence in His faithful words and to not be **afraid** to make difficult but right decisions.

He invites me to be continually encouraged by His words - "rhema" – alive and active in my spirit. Because I know that the Lord my God will be with me wherever He commands me to go.

All for His glory.

Joshua 1:9
Have I not commanded you? Be strong and courageous.
Do not be afraid; do not be discouraged, for the LORD
your God will be with you wherever you go."

As this fearless journey continues,
I know, that the Lord my God holds
me with His right hand.

L→R: Maria Theresa, her son Immanuel John and her youngest daughter Stephanie Joy

Maria Theresa with her eldest daughter Elizabeth Irene

MARIA THERESA TRONO-LEGIRALDE

Maria Theresa Trono-Legiralde is the third of five children of Dr. Gavino C. Trono Jr. and Mrs. Leticia B. Trono. She has two elder brothers – Edgar and Romeo and is the eldest among three girls; her sisters Maria Josephine and Maria Aloha Leilani (the youngest passed away in 2015).

Her elementary years up to second year high school were spent in Manila Central University. For her third-year high school she was accepted at the U.P. (University of the Philippines) High School, now U.P. Integrated School. She graduated with a Bachelor of Science in Fisheries, major in Inland Fisheries, UP College of Fisheries in Diliman Quezon City. She finished her Master of Science in Aquaculture, Major in Fish Nutrition, from the UP Visayas, Miagao, Iloilo in 1988.

She has 15 years of government service under the Technology and Livelihood Resource Center as technical consultant, project appraiser/ evaluator and in her private capacity as a technical trainer for selected aquaculture training courses. After a government offer for an early retirement plan, she moved on to work for the Meralco Foundation Inc. for five years, 2005-2010.

She migrated to New Zealand in October 2010 and happily lives with her children. She recently finished her online studies in project management.

She accepted Christ as her Lord and Savior when she was in the U.P. High School.

Her journey as a believer of Jesus Christ, is a testament of the truth of God in Psalm 100:5:

> *"For the LORD is good and his love endures forever;*
> *his faithfulness continues through all generations."*

CHAPTER 6
7 DEADLY FEARS AND HOW TO OVERCOME THEM
Ground Zero and Three Ultimate Antidotes to FEAR
By Jackie Morey

"Such love has no fear, because perfect love expels all fear."
~1 John 4:18 NLT

Who hasn't heard of the word "phobia"? It's the Greek word which means "fear".

Phobia is dictionary-defined as an *extreme or irrational fear or an aversion to something.*

When I did a quick search for different types of fears or phobias, I was shocked at how many there were!!

Did you know that **Pteromerhanophobia** is the word for the fear of flying?

And did you know that **Mageirocophobia** is the word for the fear of cooking?

Have you heard of **Chronomentrophobia** – the fear of clocks?

Or **Barophobia** – which is the fear of gravity?

Flying in planes, cooking, clocks and gravity are things I personally *don't* fear.

But my goodness, I'm grieved to think that there are people who actually fear these things!

One morning, my daughter came to me and said, "Mom, I *hate* Math!"

I was taken aback because "hate" is such a strong word, and we've encouraged our children to use the phrase "really don't like" or the word "dislike" instead of the word *hate*.

I asked, "What's wrong? What happened?"

She promptly replied, "I just don't like Math because I *hate* making mistakes!"

Ahhhhh…now we're getting somewhere.

After my daughter and I talked a bit more, I discovered the root of this "hatred" of Math – and it was the fear of making mistakes…in other words, the **fear of failure**.

There's actually an underlying cause for the fear of failure, and **my promise** to you is that we'll talk about this in a few moments.

As I write this chapter during the Spring of 2021, millions if not billions of people worldwide are gripped and crippled by the fear of getting infected with the covid-19 virus. It has caused intense despair, pandemonium, and fear on an *unprecedented* **global** scale!

The bottom line is people are fearful of getting sick from this virus, and ultimately are afraid that they could die because of this.

After a brief analysis, we could say that the *two fears* related to this covid virus are: the fear of illness (also known as **hypochondria**) and the fear of death (also known as **necrophobia**).

When I was a child, I remember that I began to fear the dark, right after my grandparents whom I was spending the weekend with, had chosen to watch a very scary horror movie!

Oh, how I hated that feeling of fear. After the movie ended, I felt terrified, scared, and did not look forward to going to sleep by myself in one of their rooms with the lights off!

After I clambered onto my bed that night, I couldn't sleep for the longest time.

My eyes were wide open, my heart beat faster, and even when sleep was causing my eyelids to get heavier by the second, I *refused* to close my eyes.

Essentially, I was on high alert – all because I feared that there was either that same "floating head without a body", or the headless body hidden behind the doors of my closet that I had just seen on TV that night.

Ugh!

Nyctophobia is the fear of the dark.

Phasmophobia is the fear of ghosts *or* other supernatural entities.

Thankfully, I've successfully overcome *both* the fear the dark **and** the fear of ghosts as a teenager.

Here's the point.

We have *all* experienced **fear** of some sort, at some point in our lives.

Now, let's presuppose that you and I are highly productive and mature adults. Given this presupposition, I'd like to have a conversation around what I consider as "Seven Deadly Fears."

You and I both know that there are *many* other fears, more than just seven.

But I consider these seven fears as "deadly" because they could actually *deter* us from cultivating our fullest potential, can *stop us in our tracks* from living out the very destinies that we were created for, or completely *derail* us from our divinely designed lives.

Let's talk about these fears one by one, **not in any order of priority**.

The First Deadly Fear – The Fear of Failure

The Fear of Failure is also called **Atychiphobia**.

According to my research, the fear of failure is one of the most common fears. It not only encompasses the fear of personal failure, but also things such as the fear of financial ruin, and the fear of unemployment.

This fear of failure can become so debilitating that it thwarts a person from undertaking *any* goal wherein success is *not* guaranteed. This results in holding people back from new experiences and opportunities – that could very well be part of their God-ordained destinies.

Keeping My Promise: As **promised** earlier, let's talk about the fear of failure, and what could be causing this fear in the first place.

Why would a person be afraid to make a mistake and be afraid to fail, when we all fail at one point or another, we live in a broken, fallen world – and *no one is perfect*, except GOD?

Well, the underlying cause of the fear of failure is actually the **fear of embarrassment** or the **fear of public humiliation**. That is at the root of the **fear of failure**.

You see, underneath the fear of making mistakes/fear of failure that our daughter was experiencing when she claimed, "I hate Math!" was the fear of public embarrassment. She dreaded the possibility of making mistakes in case some other person might find out about these mistakes, and she feared being ridiculed, taunted and looked down upon.

Can you see how the fear of embarrassment or public humiliation is what undergirds the fear of failure?

While we were having lunch together recently, my husband Jim had a powerful, insightful A-ha moment. Here's the powerful insight he shared with me:

> **"The ramifications and consequences of the fear of failure are far worse than the failure itself."**
> **~Jim Morey**

Allow me to explain.

Did you know that living one's life day in and day out in fear can actually cause physical illness?

Many studies have shown that when a person is filled with worry, anxiety and fear, these affect the person's physical body and mental well-being, and eventually could manifest through a disease.

Research by the University of Minnesota shows that fear weakens our immune system and can cause ulcers, cardiovascular damage, fatigue, clinical depression, accelerated aging, gastrointestinal problems, decreased fertility and even premature death. Fear also affects our brain processing and long-term memories, damages certain parts of our brain, and negatively impacts our thinking and decision-making.

So you see, the *consequences* of fear are indeed far worse than what is feared in the first place.

My husband Jim has a friend from his former church community, let's call him Ned (not his real name). Ned is paralyzed by the fear of failure, and at the root, he's crippled by the fear of public embarrassment.

Instead of taking the time to learn new skills or study a course at a technical school to improve himself so that he could get promoted or increase his earning capacity, Ned – now in his 50s – is stuck at a dead-end, minimum wage job at a grocery store near his apartment.

You would be astonished to know that Ned has *never* ventured outside a **10-mile radius** of his apartment!

Ned emails Jim every now and then, conveying that he'd like to enroll in some classes. But over the years that he's said this, Ned has consistently bailed out of his plan at the last minute, and has never followed through.

Why?

Because he is so fearful that he might flunk the class. And in his heart and mind, that "failure" would result in his public humiliation.

The Second Deadly Fear – The Fear of Change

Metathesiophobia is the Fear of Change.

This fear is closely related with **Tropophobia**, which is the fear of moving. This is prevalent in those whose families, or who themselves were moved *constantly* and *often* from one home to another, when they were young children.

In other words, this fear rises up in those who had to be repeatedly uprooted from one house to another, which resulted in much *instability* during their formative years.

Why do people fear change?

It's because of the instability they experienced in their childhood. In their minds and emotions, they have an equation. To them…

Change = Loss

You see, whenever they moved and changed addresses, they likely lost contact with family members, classmates, neighbors, close friends. To a child, these are huge losses.

And even when *different* kinds of changes occur, they still associate these changes with pain, suffering and hardship.

As you and I know, change is *constant*.

And we know that with good change, yes, there may be some loss, but ultimately, the "good change" far outweighs the losses.

Because with good change also comes more **opportunities** to develop new personal friendships, new business relationships, become part of new communities, and hopefully, more satisfaction and success according to that person's definition.

People with **metathesiophobia** feel as though they have zero control over their lives because of all the *many* changes that do occur in life as a general rule.

This is why metathesiophobes will rarely veer from their established routines. They stay within that comfort zones and as a consequence, they stifle their own growth and productivity, and thus, are derailed from their divinely designed destinies.

Just watch the news…change *is* constant!

Ok, wait – on second thought, perhaps just read about the news online and you'll know how much change happens from one day to the next.

Now, in spite of the reality that *change is constant*, it is **vital** that during children's formative years, they are "planted" in environments where they can grow roots, thrive and bloom.

When this kind of environment is *not* provided, these children grow into adults with varying levels of the **fear of change**.

Shockingly, because change *is* part and parcel of living in this world, **metathesiophobia** has been known to **reduce a person's will to live!**

How and why?

Well, metathesiophobes are simply unwilling to change anything from their routines, unwilling to move or make progress.

Can you imagine what this does? It severely impacts their personal and professional lives!

Remember Ned? This is exactly what has happened to him – both his personal life *and* his professional life have been completely derailed because the fear of change has crippled him.

It's heart-wrenching to know that he has *never* ventured outside the **10-mile radius** of his apartment.

The Third Deadly Fear – The Fear of Rejection

The Fear of Rejection can be classified as a *social anxiety disorder* **or** *social phobia*.

A person with this phobia feels intense anxiety and an uncontrollable fear when they are around everyday people such as cashiers, a worker at a store, being at a party, or other social situations.

This causes those with this social phobia to avoid social situations altogether.

A more dreadfully severe case of this fear of rejection is called **Anthropophobia**.

Those with anthropophobia will exhibit the same symptoms as those with social anxiety, but they will also exhibit symptoms even in instances *completely unrelated* to social interactions.

Antrhopophobia is beyond the scope of what I'd like to cover in this book, so I'll focus on the Fear of Rejection related to social phobia or social anxiety disorder.

Let me share a personal anecdote.

Although I don't believe I've ever had social anxiety disorder, I can vividly remember my freshman year in high school when I felt a lot of anxiety and dread.

I was a Catholic back then, and prior to high school, I had previously attended a *private*, all-girls Catholic school throughout all my years in grade school.

When I passed the entrance exam to the University of the Philippines High School (yes, this State university also ran its own high school), my parents decided that I was done with grade school and ready for this *co-ed public high school*.

Gulp.

Oh, what an incredibly rude awakening it was for me during my first week at school with not only girl classmates, but also **boy classmates**! **Boys**!

Sure, these boys were smart, otherwise, they wouldn't have passed the entrance exam. Some were decent. But most were also very active, rambunctious, and loud. Several were mischievous, some were smart alecs, a few were downright disrespectful to some of our teachers, and a handful sadly got into drugs and alcohol.

Imagine this…a prim and proper Catholic girl like me, who was used to a peaceful, quiet school wherein we all walked in single file from our classroom to the cafeteria, or from our classroom to the chapel and back, a school filled with respectful classmates and schoolmates – and then all of a sudden, I was *thrust* into **this** kind of school – a *co-ed public school with loud, mischievous boys!*

I felt terribly out of place, especially because I had very little social skills back then to interact with these types of guys!

What made matters worse is that some of the guys would label some guys *and* girls with derogatory names. Surprisingly, they never bothered to pick on me, likely because I was too much "inside my shell" during that freshman year.

The high school allowed girls to wear either navy pants or navy skirts as part of our uniform. Well, one week, a few of the guys attached mirrors to the end of their shoes so that they could peek from below, at some of the girls who wore skirts. Ewww!! I was horrified!!

One of my female classmates told me that these guys were called into the principal's office that same week…whew.

I distinctly remember that only a couple of months into the school year, I seriously felt sick to my stomach and *fearful* every morning, about going to school. I dreaded school, I wanted out, and I felt like quitting school every single day for several more months as a freshman.

Sigh.

Thankfully, I made friends with a few girls in my class, and got to know some of my guy classmates that year. I began to feel more at ease being at this public high school. My feelings of dread and fear slowly dissipated and eventually disappeared altogether before the end of my freshman year.

By the time I became a sophomore, I had gained much more confidence, I'd come out of my shell, I'd cultivated more social skills – especially my communication skills with guys, and I overcame the fear of rejection, thank the LORD.

The Fourth Deadly Fear – The Fear of Abandonment

Athazagoraphobia is the Fear of Abandonment.

It also includes the fear of forgetting someone, the fear of being forgotten, the fear of being ignored, and the *fear of being abandoned*.

According to research, this Fear of Abandonment usually stems from loss during one's early childhood – typically a traumatic event such as the death of a parent, or the loss of a parent through divorce, or not getting enough physical or emotional care as a child.

In an article from the Pew Research Center published on March 9, 2017, according to data from the U.S. Census Bureau and the National Center for Health Statistics, astoundingly, the divorce rate among U.S. adults 50 and over roughly *doubled* since the 1990s.

Even more staggering, is that the data showed that among those 65 years and older, the divorce rate ***roughly tripled*** since the 1990s!

Given that the divorce rate combined with undeclared separations and legal separation cases are at an all-time high not only here in the United States but in many other countries, the chances of an adult having experienced traumatic losses in early childhood or even in their teens, is fairly high.

As a result, these early childhood experiences could lead to a fear of being abandoned by other people later in life.

Would you like to know *some* symptoms of someone who has abandonment issues?

Well – i) they push others away for fear of being rejected and eventually being abandoned; ii) they have an *inability* to trust others; iii) they are "people pleasers"; iv) they feel insecure in romantic relationships and/or friendships; v) they need to control others; vi) they remain in unhealthy relationships; and also vii) they give way too much in relationships.

Now, just because someone exhibits one or more of these symptoms doesn't necessarily mean that they have the fear of abandonment. These symptoms might be caused by other fears, such as the fear of rejection.

Those gripped by the fear of abandonment have an underlying fear that they will lose important people in their life. Hence, they will sabotage relationships by saying something or doing something that will push away the other person.

Those crippled by this fear won't be able to fully trust others, not even those divinely sent their way, to help them.

Can you see how this fear could be a huge deterrent to fulfilling one's God-given destiny?

Many years ago, I had a friend who exhibited many of the above symptoms. I witnessed his tears flow freely when he didn't get the time he had expected with a close friend, because that friend was going away for a weekend trip.

It was sad for our group of friends to see him in this condition.

The Fifth Deadly Fear – The Fear of the Future

Chronophobia is The Fear of the future.

In theory, we know that fear and worry about the future is *not only* a waste of time but also an exercise in futility.

I've heard someone say that **worry** is "borrowing tomorrow's problems *today*."

Isn't that so powerful and true?

The **fear of the future**, **worry**, or borrowing tomorrow's problems today – doesn't sound like a very good nor smart thing to do, does it?

7 DEADLY FEARS AND HOW TO OVERCOME THEM

And yet the temptation to become *fearful* is very real when a natural disaster occurs, or a loved one is terminally ill, or someone loses their job.

The propensity to *worry* is very real when a spouse announces that they filed for divorce, or a business partner swindles the other partners, or your teenage or adult child is addicted to drugs and alcohol.

In these instances, it is as though the rug has been pulled out from under you!

A few years ago, my Husband Jim was let go from his job with no explanation given whatsoever. There was no two-week notice, no one-week notice, nothing. This experience had never happened to my Husband before, so he was quite astonished and felt as though the rug had indeed been pulled out from under him!

When he came home and told me, I was shocked!

I'll share with you very soon how I responded to this.

The Sixth Deadly Fear – The Fear of the Unknown

Xenophobia is The Fear of the Unknown.

Some think that xenophobia is merely the fear of strangers and different cultures, when it actually encompasses *much more* than this.

According to Healthline.com, researchers define xenophobia as *"the tendency to be afraid of something you have no information about on any level."*

Some people thrive under uncertain circumstances, while others would completely buckle under these same circumstances and become emotionally crippled.

For those with xenophobia, unknown circumstances could cause their heart rates to increase rapidly, their muscles to tighten, their breathing to become shallow, they feel intensely anxious, and they feel that these circumstances are "unbearable."

Have you met or heard about people, who at the end of their lives have shared their regrets – regarding things they wished they had done, places they wished they had visited or lived in, and people they wished they had restored or deepened their relationships with?

Life is full of unknowns, and *no* human being can have *all* the information about *everything* regarding their individual life.

And so to live life to your fullest, God-given potential, you must overcome the fear of the unknown, be willing to step into the unknown, and become fearless.

Yes, I know, I know – this is easier said than done.

Remember that I'll share with you the three Ultimate Antidotes to fear very soon.

The Seventh Deadly Fear – The Fear of Success

Achievemephobia is The Fear of Success.

This fear is interesting to me because it *doesn't* necessarily mean that the person experiencing this fear is an unsuccessful individual.

That said, it could also be experienced by those who are *not* successful at all.

For the purpose of this book, let's discuss **Achievemephobia** in the context of a group of people who have *already* reached a measure of success – according to the world's standards.

As we apply it to this more defined group of people, what the fear of success means is that these people are already successful, but they are fearful of their *next* level of success, or the *next*, *next* level of success.

In other words, they've placed a self-imposed ceiling **or** a cap on their success.

Now, why would they be fearful if they've already reached a measure of success?

From my own research, it's because of these possible factors [this is only a partial list of some potential reasons]:

1. They fear that they *can't* handle the next level of responsibilities, they *can't* manage a larger team or a bigger playing field, and that this next level might cause them personal and/or professional failure.
2. They may get much more public attention than they desire, and they are very uncomfortable dealing with this kind of extra attention, or personally do not want such attention.
3. They feel as though they're already "juggling so many plates in the air", that they fear all or most of these plates would come crashing down, instead of creatively thinking of solutions on how to manage a bigger playing field.

4. The Impostor Syndrome – though it is not considered a psychiatric diagnosis, the Impostor Syndrome is when Person A thinks that once they reach the *next* level of success, others will think that Person A is a fraud, or that Person A doesn't deserve it.
5. They fear that they're not strong enough to handle the criticism of others at this next level of success. In other words, it's the *fear of judgment* by others.

Many success-and-leadership magazine articles, news articles, lifestyle articles, and mental health magazine articles have been written about this fear.

Research shows that many entrepreneurs have experienced the fear of success.

One sobering and pithy statement by the late Stephen Covey – an American educator, bestselling author of "The 7 Habits of Highly Effective People", businessman and keynote speaker – has greatly impacted me ever since I read it back in the early 90s:

> **"Most people spend their whole lives climbing the ladder of success only to realize, when they get to the top, the ladder has been leaning against the wrong wall."**

I wonder if the above truth has caused many people to "fear success" because getting to their next level of success could potentially be yet another rung on the "wrong ladder" – which would get them to the wrong place even faster.

According to Author E.B. Johnson:

> *"...fear of success is a very real and very pervasive thing that can dramatically undermine your happiness. When we suffer from a fear of success, we self-sabotage and turn away from opportunities that might otherwise offer us rewarding experiences and fulfillment."*

Before we move on to the next fear, I'd like to offer some solutions to the #3 factor above regarding "juggling so many plates in the air."

Instead of worrying and staying fearful about more "juggling" when they get to the next level of success, some solutions are:

a) Have open and deep conversations about this next level of success with the most important people in their lives – their family and closest friends;

b) Collaborate with other people, such as those in their current team(s) or department(s);

c) Outsource some or most of the added responsibilities;

d) Delegate the "heavier work load" to existing team members who are hungry and are eager for more work – and eventually promote them;

e) Hire more team members.

Can you see how thinking creatively and thinking "outside of the box" could easily alleviate whatever angst we feel about the next level of success?

The fear of success can greatly impact both entrepreneurs, successful business people and successful team members alike.

Has this specific fear ever prevented you from moving to *your* next level of success?

Before we talk about **Ground Zero and Three Ultimate Antidotes to Fear,** I promised that I'd share how I responded to the time when my husband was let go from work with no explanation given.

It happened a little after 930am one morning, while I was in our master bedroom, *on the phone* with a dear friend, praying.

All of a sudden, Jim came through the door and announced to me that he had just been laid off, with no reason given, no 2-week notice, no warning whatsoever!

My jaw dropped and my eyes became as large as saucers! I promptly shared this shocking news with my friend who was on hold on the phone, and she, too, expressed her utter astonishment!

In that moment, I could have *easily* gone from shock…into worry-anxiety-and-fear mode. Easily.

But because my friend and I had already been praying regarding Jim's career for several months, and we were mature Christ-followers, we instead went into full-blown mountain-moving faith mode!!

We knew that this shocking situation had been allowed into our lives, after it had already been filtered through the loving Hands of a good Father, a loving God.

My friend and I promptly and fervently prayed: We asked the Lord for wisdom for Jim regarding his next steps, for favor as he applied for work positions, for strength and grace for the both of us, and for the Lord's faithful provision for our family while Jim was job-searching.

Please know that I'm not sharing this to brag. No, not at all.

I'm sharing this because I want to let you know what's possible.

When something happens that makes it seem as though "the rug was pulled out from under you" you don't have to go into fear or panic mode whatsoever.

No.

Instead, you, my dear Reader – can begin your journey to become FEARLESS!!

Ground Zero

Ok, here we are. Ground Zero.

The buck stops here, so please take heed to what I'm about to share.

I guarantee you that you *cannot* overcome any of the fears I listed above *without* these very important **two steps**.

Are you ready? Ok, here it is…

If you truly want to become *fearless*, the **first step in Ground Zero** – and one of the first and most important decisions you'll ever make is this:

Acknowledge all the traumatic incidents and events that you've experienced.

Yes, I know that this first step in and of itself could be very painful.

How do I know?

Because I've been there. I have personally experienced several traumas in my life, and the first step I took so that I could become who I am today, was to *acknowledge* that I had been traumatized.

Now the next step in Ground Zero is *more* excruciating, but I promise you, it will be well worth it.

Step Two is very important because this step will impact you for the rest of your life, the lives of your immediate family members, and the generations that follow.

Ok, **the second step in Ground Zero**: **Choose to seek help for your complete healing from the trauma you've experienced.**

Yes, you must decide to reach out to others who can actually help you get healed, restored, and delivered. There are people that the Lord has for you, who can help you.

You are not alone. Please don't cut this journey short or rob yourself of your full healing and restoration.

This is one of the most important and crucial decisions you'll ever make because from this decision, your life will never be the same.

You're right. This could take weeks, months…perhaps even years.

When you seek help to get healed from trauma, this extraordinary investment will reap massive benefits for you – and the ROI is *priceless*.

Many, many years ago, I finally acknowledged that I needed help, that I needed healing, and so I took the next step of seeking help.

I went to a Licensed Mental Health Therapist who was a Christ-follower. She helped me through three (3) different traumatic incidents that occurred at different stages in my life.

My painfully-good journey from trauma to healing took over 2-1/2 years. And I can authentically tell you that it was *well worth* all of the pain, and the entire gamut of emotions that I experienced during that season of my life.

My story is that the Lord healed and restored me as completely as possible this side of heaven – praise GOD!! And though I may have scars, I am healed and the traumas are no longer massive, gaping, open, bloody emotional wounds like they were when I first started.

Please don't think for one moment that you can skip the steps in Ground Zero.

Has anyone ever built a house without a foundation?

Ground Zero is your foundation.

Several years ago, I read the breaking news about a pastor of a mega-church in Florida who suddenly resigned because he had become an alcoholic and had to admit it to his congregation.

This incredible man had worked very hard to build up this mega-church with thousands of members, excellent worship teams, a TV show, book series, and more.

At the end of the news article, he shared that when he finally reached a level of success, the accompanying level of the pressure and stress from the ministry caused him to implode emotionally, break down, and to turn to alcohol – all because of the undealt, unhealed childhood molestation and abuse he suffered as a young boy.

Wow.

The pressure and stress from his ministry *merely magnified* all the gaping emotional wounds, mental stress, and the excruciating, undealt-with pain he had suffered.

He felt so much shame and guilt that he "hid under the rug" all the horrific abuse for those many years, just to keep up with his growing success.

You see, without going through and establishing a firm foundation at Ground Zero, I truly believe that in the end, whatever "success" you build will eventually come *crashing down*.

It would be like building your house upon sand.

Ground Zero is foundational.

Three Ultimate Antidotes to FEAR

Are you ready to conquer fear in your life?

Are you committed to the journey of become FEARLESS?

Have you completed the two-step Ground Zero process?

Excellent.

Then you're ready for the three Ultimate Antidotes to FEAR.

1. The Growth Mindset
2. Choose Faith Over Fear
3. Perfect Love

The Growth Mindset

Ultimate Antidote #1 is The Growth Mindset.

What in the world is the growth mindset?

In Dr. Carol Dweck's groundbreaking and brilliant bestselling book "Mindset", she discovered that people who had the best potential to flourish and experience long-term success were those who had a **growth mindset** as opposed to those who had a **fixed mindset**.

Here's a short comparison list of the difference between those who have a fixed mindset vs. those who have a growth mindset.

Fixed Mindset	**Growth Mindset**
I'm afraid of making a mistake.	Mistakes are how I learn and get better.
I don't like challenges.	Challenges make me better!
I'm not good at this.	What can I learn to get better a this?

I can't do it.	I'm still learning. I'll keep trying!
It's too hard.	With more practice, it will get easier!
I don't know how.	I can learn how!
I give up.	I'll try a different way!

What a stark contrast between these two mindsets, right?!

I'd like to hone in for a moment on the fear-based, fixed mindset first line: *I'm afraid of making a mistake.*

Remember how we talked about the Fear of Failure earlier?

Well, *wouldn't* it be truly game-changing, if instead of the above fear-based, fixed mindset, we could *purposefully and intentionally* make the following belief statement *our automatic default*?

"Mistakes are how I learn and get better!"

Can you see how we need to rewire our brains, to *change* the way we think – from being *fearful* and thinking small…into having a **growth mindset**?

Remember, no one is served by you thinking small.

In the Word of God, we are called to be transformed by renewing of our minds…by *changing* the way we think. (Check out Romans 12:2)

The Growth Mindset has indeed transformed millions of people for the better.

If you are serious about your journey toward becoming *fearless*, I highly recommend getting Carol Dweck, PhD.'s book – **Mindset**. Here's the link for your convenience:

7 DEADLY FEARS AND HOW TO OVERCOME THEM   121

(Photo from Jackie Morey's personal vault)

https://amzn.to/3fwGI23

Also, I recommend that you invest in a comparison chart such as this:

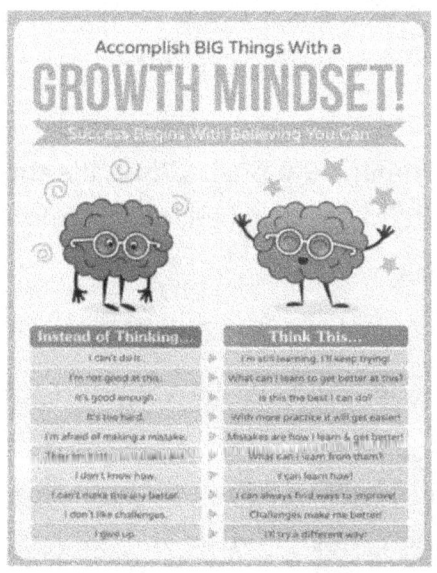

(Photo from Jackie Morey's personal vault)

https://amzn.to/3ubs4Tn

If you are committed to becoming fearless, I invite you to avail of **Ultimate Antidote #1 – The Growth Mindset**.

Ok, let's move on to Ultimate Antidote #2.

Choose Faith Over Fear

Ultimate Antidote #2 is to Choose Faith Over Fear.

When I did a search on the phrase "Faith Over Fear," I was pleasantly surprised that not only faith-based websites were listed, but also articles from Wheaton College, a Registered Nurses' organization, and the University of Pennsylvania.

I propose that faith is not just for "religious" people.

How and why is **faith** an antidote to *fear*?

First of all, faith is the opposite of fear.

When your heart-posture and your mind are anchored in faith, fear is automatically pushed out. It's similar to dark and light. When a light is switched on, it automatically dispels darkness!

That's why when you choose faith, it dispels fear.

Secondly, faith is *not* some utopian illusion.

The Word of God says: *"Faith is the confidence that what we hope for will actually happen; it gives us assurance about things we cannot see."* ~Hebrews 11:1 NLT

For faith-based people, **faith** is the confidence, substantial belief and whole-hearted trust in an all-powerful, all-loving, omniscient, and omnipresent Supernatural Being who has their highest good in mind. One who can and *does* rescue, heal, guide, provide, and support us through whatever comes our way.

Fear, on the other hand – causes us to focus on the negative circumstances surrounding us, believe that things could only get worse, that we are isolated and alone, and that there is no such thing as a divinely designed solution or divinely orchestrated help.

The interesting thing is that both faith *and* fear are defined as *believing in something*.

Faith is believing in something / Someone we can't see, we can't hear with our ears, touch with our hands, smell with our noses, or taste with our taste buds.

Fear is *also* believing in something we can't see, something that hasn't happened yet, or may never even happen to begin with.

The major difference is, faith *empowers* and *lives in the light* – whereas fear completely *disempowers*, and *feeds on darkness*.

There are millions of testimonies of people from all walks of life who can tell you that their *faith* in GOD sustained them, lifted them up, delivered their loved ones from addictions, caused them to receive miraculous answers to prayer, caused them to receive financial miracles, resulted in their physical and emotional healing – and so much more!!

Faith is an extraordinarily powerful force because it's "direct Object" – so to speak, is an omnipotent, omnipresent, omniscient, supernatural Being who has always wanted a huge family.

Faith is the opposite of fear.

Faith is the antidote to fear.

It's ultimately your choice what you choose.

I invite you to choose faith.

I invite you to avail of Antidote #2 – Choose Faith Over Fear.

Perfect Love

Ultimate Antidote #3 is Perfect Love.

You've likely heard this scripture at a wedding or read it somewhere:

"Three things will last forever – faith, hope, and love – and the greatest of these is love." ~1 Corinthians 13:13 NLT

…The greatest of these is **love**.

Why do I believe that *perfect love* is one of three ultimate antidotes to fear?

Well, there's a powerful ancient scripture that states:

"There is no fear in love. But perfect love drives out fear, because fear has to do with punishment. The one who fears is not made perfect in love." ~1 John 4:18 (emphasis mine)

Did you see that?!

Perfect love <u>drives out</u> fear!!

In other words, "Adios muchachos, bye-bye to fear!!"

Wow.

Would you like to experience this perfect love which could drive out any and all fear from your life?

Great!

Before that, let's first establish: What is this *perfect love* and where does it come from?

It's actually the *ultimate love*, the unconditional, relentless love that originates from the Great I Am, the God of Abraham, Isaac and Jacob, Yahweh, the One whom the Lord Jesus Christ called Abba – when He taught His disciples the "Lord's Prayer."

His *perfect love* pursues the "worst" of people and transforms murderers like Pharisee Saul into the apostle Paul…

…witches and warlocks into powerful, enemies-to-darkness Christ-followers

…hardened criminals into caring and responsible individuals who minister to gang members

…drug addicts and alcoholics into sober, selfless adults who mentor others get out of their addictions

…and He transforms people from all walks of life who acknowledge that they, too, are sinners – into children of God!!

Not only does Father God's **perfect love** transform lives, on a very practical level, it can also *dispels fear* in your life and mine.

According to World Population Review – an independent organization without political affiliations – as of 2021,

Christianity is the world's largest religion, practiced by 2.38 billion people.

Any single one of these 2.38 billion Christians – who has declared that Yeshua Ha Mashiach (Jesus the Messiah) is their personal Lord and Savior, who knows that their sins have been washed away and fully paid for by the Blood of Jesus and the finished work of Jesus Christ on the cross – can avail of and experience this **perfect love** from the One whom we can now call "our Heavenly Father", Papa, Daddy, Abba.

And when you have experienced this *perfect love* from Abba/the Lord Jesus/the Holy Spirit – emergency situations, tragic circumstances, national disasters, "global pandemics", demons, challenging relationship issues, etc. ***may tempt*** you to fear…but you ***do not*** have to give in to that temptation.

Instead, simply connect with Yahweh (Our Heavenly Father), or with Yeshua (Jesus), or with Ruach Ha Kodesh (the Holy Spirit), and receive another fresh in-filling of this *perfect love*.

Personally, I need Abba's *perfect love* every single day so that I can be the best wife, mother, sister, friend, entrepreneur and neighbor.

And because of this, no matter what emergency situation, crisis, challenge or relationship issues arise, I have rarely gone into fear mode.

I remember the night before my Husband's scheduled surgery on July 10, 2020.

Due to covid restrictions, I couldn't take our children to visit him at the hospital.

Thankfully, that night, my kids and I were able to video-chat with Jim.

Our kids were asleep in their rooms, and I was laying alone in our king-sized bed.

I remember how I was tempted to *worry*. I was tempted to *fear the future*. I was tempted to get *anxious* about how the surgery would go the next day. I was tempted to *worry* about Jim's health after surgery.

Well, there's a *powerful* ancient scripture that I promptly implemented:

"Don't worry about anything; instead, pray about everything. Tell God what you need, and thank him for all he has done. Then you will experience God's peace, which exceeds anything we can understand. His peace will guard your hearts and minds as you live in Christ Jesus." ~Philippians 4:6-7 NLT

So for the rest of the night before I fell asleep, and during the couple of times I woke up in the middle of the night – I prayed for, interceded, declared and decreed on behalf of Jim, the surgeons and nurses involved with the upcoming surgery, our children and myself.

Candidly, I can testify that I experienced God's supernatural peace over me *that night*, the next day, and long after Jim was discharged from the hospital.

I truly sensed God's ***perfect love*** which **drove out fear**...wow – thank You, LORD!!

Do you want to become fearless? Are you truly committed to this?

Then I invite you to to *fully avail* of Ultimate Antidote #3 – Perfect Love – which comes from Abba, our Heavenly Father.

Allow me to summarize everything we talked about.

Seven Deadly Fears that could derail someone's destiny are:

1. The Fear of Failure
2. The Fear of Change
3. The Fear of Rejection
4. The Fear of Abandonment
5. The Fear of the Future
6. The Fear of the Unknown
7. The Fear of Success

The Journey to Become Fearless

If you want to become fearless, here's a quick equation to remember so that you can successfully overcome these fears:

How to Overcome FEAR = Ground Zero + Three Ultimate Antidotes to Fear

Ground Zero is a two-step process.

And the Three Ultimate Antidotes to Fear are:

1. The Growth Mindset
2. Choose Faith Over Fear
3. Perfect Love

Important Note: The above equation is *not* some quick-fix formula. Instead, it is an effective way to remember vital steps and processes that are part and parcel of **the journey to become fearless**.

Well, my dear Reader – I hope you thoroughly enjoyed reading this chapter and gained massive value and powerful insights.

Please share this chapter with others and connect with me if you have any stories, praise reports and testimonies regarding your journey to become fearless.

Last but not least, I ask that you kindly rate this book on Amazon, preferably give us a 5-star review, please.

Thank you very, very much!

Christmas Day 2020
Jim and Jackie, Michael and Alyssa

JACKIE LANSANGAN-MOREY

Jackie is a premier entrepreneur, 9-time #1 International Bestselling Author, Book Publisher, Editor, Virtual Book Launch Host/Consultant, and Prophetic Mentor.

She's also a WebTV Host and Producer of "Jackie Morey LIVE", "The 21st Century Legacy Letters", "The Exponential You", and is the Founder and CEO of Customer Strategy Academy.

Her passion is to help leaders, consultants, coaches, business professionals, medical professionals, writers and entrepreneurs – to grow their business & live their lives purposefully and by design, not by default, through her Book Writing, Editing, Book Publishing, and Online Marketing businesses.

As a degreed Engineer, she brings her unique logical expertise to simplify the nuts and bolts of writing, self-publishing and launching her clients to Bestselling Authors.

Jackie is a recognized Revenue-Generator, Relationship Ambassador, Topnotch Solution Provider, Creative Problem-solver, Peacemaker, and Team-builder.

She enjoys movies, gourmet dark chocolate, traveling, jazz, pop and classical music, chess, writing, bike riding, volleyball, table tennis, having coffee with family and friends, savoring sweet, juicy Philippine mangoes, snorkeling in the tropical beaches of Coron, Palawan, and sharing prophetic words with and for family members, friends, and occasionally, with complete strangers as the Lord leads.

She's happily married and lives in a beautiful Pacific Northwest suburb of Seattle with her husband Jim. They have a son and a daughter who "make them proud" every day.

Connect with Jackie:
Facebook: www.facebook.com/JackieMorey77
LinkedIn: www.linkedin.com/in/jackiemorey1
Twitter: www.Twitter.com/JackieMorey1

CHAPTER 7
A LEG TO STAND ON
How to Live Without Excuses,
Be Unstoppable, and Choose to
Thrive After Losing a Limb
By James R. Morey

(Excerpts from James R. Morey's #1
Bestselling book "A Leg To Stand On")

This is the story of a below the knee amputation (BKA) of my left leg. Most of the content is aimed at BKA and AKA amputees, but a good portion is also relevant to upper limb amputees, and family members.

But more importantly, this is more a story of challenge and hope, that it relevant to *everyone*.

This is a story of hope, not tragedy. It's a story of challenges not roadblocks. Molehills, not mountains.

It's my story, but it might also be *your* story.

Perhaps your story is about to start, has already started, or you're a pro. We share an experience, elements of a common story, and we can all learn from each other, gain strength from each other, be encouraged together.

Maybe you're *not* an amputee, but a family member, friend, or a caregiver – and you want some insight, hope, encouragement, or some advice from someone who *has* gone through it.

Whoever you are, whatever role you're playing in the story, or wherever in the story you are, I hope that you'll gain insight, understanding, hope, encouragement, and laugh a bit – because life is joyful, even if you, or a loved one, has been thrown a curveball.

My hope is that this book can help you to get your stance at the plate, keep your eye on that curveball, and knock that sucker out of the park!

A Curveball

Sometimes life throws us a curve ball.

You're late for work, and the car won't start. You need to do a presentation, your computer battery dies, and you can't find the charge cord.

Some of these curve balls are temporary challenges.

Other curveballs are permanent, *life-changing* challenges. One of these happened to me on July 10th, 2020.

We were all ready to go on a family vacation to visit some dear friends in Idaho that we hadn't seen for years. I was excited. My wife was excited. The kids were especially excited because we were taking them to a huge waterpark. We were all set to go.

The day before we were to leave, I went in to see my podiatrist. I had an infection in my left foot, probably caused by some minor injury.

The podiatrist and I had been working on this for weeks. I'd seen him several times prior.

I had some uneasiness in the back of my mind, but things seemed to be going along with some success. So, we were planning to leave for our vacation the next day.

There was some increased bleeding and some dark spots on my foot, but I didn't see that as a showstopper. I was mentally planning how to get around that issue on our trip. I could rent a walker or use crutches. But it was our only vacation all summer and I wasn't about to ruin my family's trip over this. No way…not gonna' happen!

What happened *next* was definitely one of those don't-blink-because-life-comes-at-you-quick moments.

When the podiatrist saw my left foot, he had a very worried look on his face. He called in another doctor. And together, they told me that the infection had gone into *geometric replication,* leading to **sepsis!**

There was only one way that they infection could be stopped, and I didn't like it.

They looked at me, with somber and serious looks on their faces.

The podiatrist told me plainly and seriously, "You could go on your trip, but you'd be dead by Sunday." Then they both looked at me and said, **"This infection cannot be stopped. You** *could either lose your leg, or you could lose your life. It's up to you."*

Things went from serious to *surreal* very quickly. I had to make an unpleasant but clear decision. And it didn't take long to make. I knew that the procedure had to be done. I called my beloved wife, Jackie, and told her what was going on and what was coming.

I asked Jackie to go on the trip without me – don't ruin things on my account, you know. But before the words even left me, I knew that this was *not* an option. Of course, she refused.

Our son Michael overheard the word "amputation" and got genuinely concerned.

This is one of those times where you just know that your life, and the lives of those around you, has just been altered, probably permanently.

They admitted me to the hospital next door.

The next day at 1pm, the orthopedic surgeon with the general surgeon, were both scheduled to perform a below-the-knee (BKA) amputation on my left leg.

Before they put me under, I asked the surgeon if I could say something first, and then also pray over the procedure and for everyone there. He approved my request.

First, I thanked everyone there for their expertise, their knowledge, and for taking such good care of me. Then I prayed for each of them, that Father God would give them wisdom and peace and that all would go well. Oh, I could feel the presence of Jesus in that operating room.

They gave me the anesthetic…I went out in *seconds*.

Later that day I awoke from the anesthetic with part of my left leg *gone*.

So, I was up to bat and life threw me a curveball, a life-altering permanent challenge. And I swung with *all* I had…

Practice Positivity

I remember laying on the hospital bed the day after the amputation and starting to think to myself, *"What do I do now? How do I live life now? What if (insert some negativity and fear)?"*

Almost immediately, a voice in my head said, and I believe it was inspired by God, *"I'm going to do what it takes to overcome this. I'll live life in a new light. I can do it. I got this!"*

That is positivity.

When we face the uncertainty of life, we throw our shoulders back and proclaim the best, the brightest. Think about it, since we don't **know** what will happen in the future, why not *assume* that good will happen rather than bad?

Studies have shown *over and over* that we subconsciously move our lives in the direction of our expectations. Every aspect of life that we can affect or control, we do so **in the direction** of our beliefs, or expectations.

So why not expect the best? Right?

Now, I am *not* a natural-born optimist.

In fact, I used to take pride in my natural ability to find the worst-case scenario in pretty much every situation in life. I was *so* good at it that I saw the worst that could happen and began to expect it.

I was constantly waiting for the "other shoe to drop" (no pun intended).

And guess what? The worst, or at least worse than should have happened, did happen with regularity. So much for being a pessimist.

For any of my fellow natural-born worst-case scenario pessimists, let me just say this – STOP IT RIGHT NOW!

I know that the thought of becoming a dyed-in-the-wool optimist sounds like, well, a worst-case scenario, it's really not that bad at all. In fact, you'll get to love it after a while.

Start small and work your way up. Practice being unstoppably positive for 5 minutes a day and work up from there.

Try to think and declare out loud the best when you encounter the next unknown situation. It doesn't cost a penny, and it doesn't hurt at all.

Then watch your life improve as you consistently apply positivity. It really *does* work.

Practice Gratitude

"What, practice gratitude?! I just lost a limb!"

Yes, that's true, but I'm still alive.

In my case, had I *not* had my amputation, I wouldn't be writing this book and you would not be reading it, because I would have died!

The thing with gratitude is that *it's work*. It's effort. But like weight training, it strengthens you as you apply it.

Start off just saying, *"I'm thankful to be alive."* In my case, I still have my wonderful, healthy, strong right leg and I am thankful for it.

Also, my health is *so* much better than before the amputation and I am thankful for that.

Keep practicing gratitude and it will soon become automatic. Just a part of your life.

The biggest gain is that as we practice gratitude, we become happier and healthier persons. We are more enjoyable to be around. Life is just plain better and more enjoyable.

Evict "If Only..."

There is always a temptation to start saying to ourselves, *"If only I had done..."* or *"If only the doctor had known or done..."* DON'T GO THERE. EVER.

Not only will it not make anything better, but it will actually make things worse. *"If only..."* is the enemy of our souls. It will rob us of life, health, happiness, time, and opportunity if we let it.

The proper way to deal with "If only..." is to kick its scrawny, evil, bitter ass out of our mind, health, and soul!

Gratitude is the boot that we use to do this. It's a steel-toed boot with a pointy tip. Be thankful for what you have and "If only..." takes the bus out of Dodge every time.

OK, off the soap box... for now.

Dealing with Change

As an amputee, I had to just plain say goodbye to some things. I used to run quite a bit in college. I played soccer and volleyball. I had to say "see you later" to these things. That said, I hope to get back there someday soon.

But some things I had to say goodbye to, like the simple act of getting up in the middle of the night and walking to go to the bathroom. This simply is not an option for me anymore. I must use my walker, my iWalk, or don my prosthetic leg. By the time that happens, I am now awake. And it takes time to get back to sleep…occasionally, a long while afterward.

This might sound simple and you might be saying to yourself, *"What's the big deal?"* The big deal to me is that this is for the **rest of my life**.

And there are other things like that.

I must think ahead if I want to go up and down the stairs. I can't just jump up and answer the doorbell. If I want to make myself a sandwich, I have to plan ahead, put on a mobility device, carry one thing at a time, and so on…

These things add up and sometimes the shear monotony of all the extra steps I have to take just to walk across the room can be a challenge in and of itself.

The fact is that we are constantly dealing with change.

How well we deal with change is a big determiner of how happy we are and the overall quality of our life.

I used to dislike change, probably even feared it.

I saw change as the enemy, a foe seeking to destroy me. I saw change as things getting worse. This is because I used to be a pessimist, remember?

For a pessimist, any change is "going to be bad" and the best hope is to work to keep things as they are.

This might seem crazy to a non-pessimist, but it makes perfectly good sense to those of us who are craz...I mean pessimists.

But as I experienced life more, especially after getting married to the most beautiful and amazing woman in the world and having two amazing kids, I grew to see change for what it really is – an *opportunity*.

This makes so much sense now, right?

If we never change, we will always be the same, have the same things, do the same things, and experience the same things. Where's the fun in that? We were created to grow and change.

The last 15 years have brought me amazing things – I went from 350 pounds and on the express lane towards death to my ideal weight and in great health, getting married to the most amazing woman in the universe, having two wonderful kids together, getting my dream job as a software developer, and many other gifts!

When I think about the amazing changes, I thank God for *change*.

Working Through Loss

Quite frankly, this chapter was the most difficult for me to write. To work through. In case you haven't picked it up, I'm a classic, hard-working, "deal-with-it-and move-on" type of guy. I'm not "touchy-feely" to say the least. I'm a "steady-as-you-go" man.

I once had a manager at work (Microsoft) tell me, *"Jim, if you were on fire, we wouldn't know except for the smoke."* That pretty much sums it up.

So, working through the emotional journey of loss that is part-and-parcel of having an amputation, was difficult for me. Difficult but necessary.

Fending Off Fear

Loss can come in the form of the *fear* of loss or the *feeling* of loss. It's imaginary, but it sure feels real at the time. Any life change can involve this imaginary loss, especially a change like amputation.

In my case, the amputation was caused because of an unstoppable infection, so, naturally, I had the fear that it would crop up again. Dealing with this took a lot of faith, time with God, and telling myself over and over again, "Ain't gonna' happen!"

But it also took action. **Nothing destroys fear like action.**

I studied hard to make sure I knew everything I could about infections associated with amputations. I studied nutrition. I studied exercise. I studied treatments. I suffered through three weeks of antibiotics and all the "fun" associated with that. I did what my doctor told me to do. I did everything I could to avoid a re-infection.

But it also took a revelation from God.

Romans 8:28 (NKJV) says: "And we know that ***all things*** *work together for good to those who love God, to those who are called according to His purpose.*" (emphasis mine)

All things, even an *amputation*. For *my* good.

One of the things that any major life change can produce is fear. And for men specifically, this is the fear that "I am no longer as much a man as I was." Or that I am now "half the man I used to be."

This is a real thing because a man's self-identity rests a lot on what he can do, how he provides for his family, what he can achieve.

An amputation can stoke the fires of this fear in a unique way because amputations limit mobility and a man's ability to perform.

The fear is that the limits are extensive and permanent and that those limits would reduce a man to *less than* a man.

Now, all of these things are false, as any irrational fear is, but they sure *feel* real in the muck of the moment. And my imagination could take advantage of that fear and attempt to solidify it in my mind.

So, my trick to defeating this fear, as is the case for all fear is ***action***. I worked hard to increase my mobility, to strengthen myself, to take care of myself.

I also take the time to work through the emotions and all the thoughts that come with this fear.

The conversations went something like this:

Fear: *"You're just a burden to those who care about you the most."*

Me: Those who really care about me will never see helping me as a "burden." Besides, I'm back to nearly 100% mobility and function. My dear wife and our wonderful kids love helping me. We're all stronger now. That's not a burden, it's a benefit.

Fear: *"You won't be there for your kids like you were before."*

Me: Yes, I will. More in fact, because they see me working through this whole thing and that teaches them lessons on faith and resolve that they couldn't learn *any* other way. Seeing me work through the losses helps them to do the same with faith and wisdom in ways I can't even grasp.

Fear: *"Your wife sees you as less of a man and you don't make her happy anymore."*

Me: No, she doesn't see me as less but more because I'm handling this with faith and strength. And *that's* sexy. And yes, I do make her happy because being a man isn't' about having all my parts but having a heart. And my heart is stronger than it has ever been.

Fear: *"Your colleagues won't respect you as much."*

Me: Yes, they will – more in fact because they see me being real and strong during this whole thing and they know that I'm working even harder to be there for them.

Fear: *"What will it be like when you're older? How will you even function?"*

Me: Ask me that after I finish my triathlon, jackass.

Working Through Sorrow

I am certainly no cry baby, but this whole experience has really brought me closer to my feelings, especially sorrow. And one of the things about sorrow is it can strike suddenly and at odd times.

For example, I lost my Dad about 20 years ago, my Mom about 10 years ago, and my older brother years ago. So, these occurred a while ago and I'm over them, right? Nope.

Even today, I'll be in a situation that will remind me of one of them, or that I might turn to them and say some inside joke, and they're not there. Then I'll get sad, and the tears will come.

It's the same with my leg. I miss my leg.

Once when I was watching a YouTube video on what to expect after an amputation, I just started crying, sobbing uncontrollably as waves of sorrow and loss washed over me.

Every time the doorbell rings and there's no one else to get it for me, I feel sad.

The loss is real and tangible. I don't try to "buck up" anymore. I let it happen. And equally important, I *don't* put myself down for it. I accept it as part of the healing process, part of me.

But as I said earlier, though the loss is real, there are also real benefits as I intentionally work through the loss and work with my emotions, instead of trying to keep them quiet or squelch them or sweep them under the rug. Focusing my emotions on these helps me to return to the new normal.

Take time for God

I don't know if you're a person of faith. I'm a follower of Jesus Christ.

On September 12, 1975 at 8:32 PM, I confessed my need for Jesus and began the most important relationship of my life. And like most, my life has been somewhat of a roller coaster.

There were good times, bad times, great times, sad times, and mad times. But through the whole thing, Jesus has always been there, right next to me in that roller coaster cart. He has never abandoned me, even in times when it seemed that pretty much everyone else did.

And through this whole journey of amputation and rehab, He's right there, cheering me on. He is my strength and joy.

If you've never considered Christ Jesus, please take some time to do so.

Mobility

After a leg amputation, regaining mobility is one of the *most important* goals an amputee can have.

A leg amputation is a mobility challenge, not an overall health challenge. There is a temptation to give in to a "crippled" mentality.

Constantly increasing my mobility helps keep me from this destructive mindset.

There is no reason that once I got trained on my prosthetic, that I couldn't have nearly 100% mobility. Even if I were a world-class sprinter before the amputation, I would've been set because they have sleek, cool carbon-fiber blades for that.

Mobility is also my key to becoming more *autonomous*. Increase my mobility and my world gets bigger. Increase my mobility and I increase my *confidence*.

I **refused** to get into the habit of having others do for me what I could do myself, even if it took longer and required more effort.

Yes, at first, I needed more help as I recovered from surgery and built my strength. But as I did, I added things every day that I did myself.

Most tasks were more difficult and took longer, but I strove to do all of those that I could by myself as soon as possible.

Falling and Getting Back Up

In a sense, regaining mobility after an amputation is like learning to walk all over again. And like the first time, falls happen.

It's just a part of the process and like we saw before the philosophy for falling is to keep getting up.

Your PT specialist will help you re-develop balance and that will reduce falling and might even eliminate it. Also, practicing with your mobility device definitely helps.

Falling and getting back up are a small reflection of the larger journey of dealing with an amputation, and really, life itself.

Life just plain is filled with challenges and sometimes we cruise through and sometimes we fall.

The trick is to just get back up, learn from it, and move on.

I fell, more than once. And the danger is not falling itself. ***The danger is fear***.

If, after a fall, I fear falling again and back off from life because of it, then I lose.

One of my falls was while trying to throw something away. We have a foot-operate trash bin. I was using my iWalk and lifted the iWalk to step on the foot pedal to open the can. I got off balance a bit and reached out with my elbow (both hands were full) to lean against the wall. I missed the wall and fell backwards and on my left side.

OK, no big deal. I took off the iWalk and prepared to get back up. My wife, Jackie, brought over a chair to help me. I grabbed the chair and started to get up. That's when things went wrong.

I forgot I had taken off my iWalk and tried to put weight on my left foot (which isn't there anymore) and fell again.

This time I hit my left ribs on the corner of the chair on the way down and hurt them. It took about two weeks for the soreness in my ribs to heal.

That wasn't the real problem, though. The problem was that I was fearful of throwing anything away using our trash bin. And I didn't for a while.

Eventually, I *made myself* throw something away using that same trash bin. This time, no problems.

The key to falling is to make sure that you always get back up again.

This simple statement is really a metaphor for life – I just make sure that I keep getting back up, regardless of how hard the fall.

A Word to Caregivers and Family

The journey that the amputee is on, is a challenging one, full of advances and retreats. Thank you for being there for them. Your presence and help mean more to them than they can say.

You have taken on a lot more work to support your loved one, work that could take a toll on you. So be sure to take time for yourself.

Remember that the journey is going somewhere – life as it should be.

A danger lies in your getting too used to your role as caregiver and wanting to, at some point, keep the amputee "safe."

You want to minimize falls, reach out, help, and serve the amputee.

While this is really needed in the beginning stages of this journey, as the amputee gains mobility and moves back to taking care of themselves, one of the hardest parts is to back-off and let them.

We need to follow the wisdom, *"Never do for someone what they can, and should, do for themselves."*

And sometimes it's difficult to back away and let the amputee do more and more. Not to mention that some things just take longer for the amputee to do.

But though it takes longer, letting the amputee do things for themselves is really what is best for them, *and* for you.

Resist the temptation to treat the amputee as a "cripple" and as someone who always needs your help.

Now, put the shoe on the other foot (pun intended) – do **not** allow the amputee to continually depend upon you. They should be progressing in their mobility and doing more for themselves as time goes by and it is part of your job as a caregiver or family member to make them do more.

Sometimes we need that. And we need your help to keep from treating ourselves as "cripples" too.

Remember this is a journey, not a destination, and the landscape should change as the amputee progresses. At first, they will need a lot of help, for almost everything.

As we gain more mobility, we need less help.

In the end, we should be back at full speed and doing pretty much everything we did before, if not more.

I remember the first day I was back from the hospital. I could barely do anything for myself. It was horrible!

Eventually, I was getting around better, especially when I got my iWalk [https://amzn.to/2LtGiyg]. I could then manage the stairs.

After several days, I even drove around our neighborhood! I remember how exhilarated I felt when I first drove our van, especially after weeks of being cooped up at home!

The day came when I finally got my prosthetic, and I could navigate the stairs pretty well. We, as a family, went places together – and I drove!

As I got trained on my prosthetic, my mobility improved by leaps and bounds such that I was able to eventually walk around well *without* a cane!

It is a process. And I am so thankful for those around me who helped, especially my beloved wife, Jackie.

And the journey went somewhere.

Today, I can do everything myself. I even let my wife get away for the weekend alone while I take care of our kiddos!

This process is important not only to the amputee, but for you the caregiver as well.

Remember: Amputation is a challenge *not* a life sentence. The amputation is permanent, but most of the challenges are *temporary*. And so is your job as a caregiver.

Eventually, you will step away from that role and get back to your previous role.

Don't get too attached to your caregiver role, and don't try to derive too much value from it – it's *temporary*. The more temporary, the better.

A Word to the Amputee

Amputee to amputee, let me say this -- amputation is a challenge *not* a sentence. The amputation is permanent, but most of the challenges are *temporary*.

Don't take on the identity of the reality – don't let yourself be labeled a "cripple" and don't take it on as a lifestyle.

Amputation is a speedbump in life, not the end of the road.

This is a *super* important TIP: Make *daily* mobility goals for yourself. Make progress every day.

They don't have to be big goals, but they have to be progress. You decide how *far* and how *fast*.

And don't stay stagnant…life is too precious to waste.

Be courageous and fearless. Strive to live better.

Develop a fighter's attitude. Get angry at complacency. Get motivated. Get going.

As you can tell from my conversations with *fear* earlier, I developed a 'tude. I became a fighter. I WILL win. I will *not* be beaten!

I subscribe to a periodical from the Amputee Coalition. In one issue there was an astonishing story about a guy who owned a tree service. He loved what he did.

One day he fell, and his leg got taken by the chipper. Yet within months he was back at it…climbing trees and doin' his thing *with a prosthetic!!*

Man, that is double-tough. His story really inspired me to go further, try harder, and to NEVER let myself be a "cripple".

The Lesson: Never accept anything but the best *for* yourself and never expect anything less than the best *from* yourself.

My personal goal is to do more *after* my amputation than before.

I was athletic in college and I slowed down as life went on. But I'm not going to accept that from myself. I will go *way beyond* what I was doing *before* the amputation.

I'm committed to becoming more mobile. I will get out and walk every day. I will play soccer again. I will do a 5K. And I'll train to do a mini-triathlon.

> "**The Lesson:** Never accept anything but the best *for* yourself and never expect anything less than the best *from* yourself."
>
> – James Morey

They say the best revenge is success.

The best "revenge" on your amputation is to go **beyond** where you were before and tell that amputation that it doesn't define you, limit you, or even slow you down!

The road back to normal isn't an easy one but it can be done, and you can do it!

May God be with you, Warrior!

Conclusion

Well this *has* been, and *still* is, an amazing journey in life.

I am astonished at the incredible faith and strength of my amazing wife, Jackie, and the resilience of our kiddos, Michael, and Alyssa.

I'm also blown away and very grateful for the incredible love, care, and generosity of dear friends and relatives who have lavishly given to my GoFundMe campaign, sent us checks, helped with errands, prepared and delivered meals, sent us GrubHub and DoorDash gift cards, consistently prayed for me and my family, and supported me while I worked my way through this challenge.

Indeed this has been a journey that has strengthened me physically, mentally, emotionally, and spiritually.

The bottom line is that I really *couldn't* have done it without the LORD, without my wife and children, without my extended family, our friends, and many others who were there when I needed them.

I'm *still* in process, ultimately, we all are.

I hope that you've found my story interesting and inspiring. And I hope that the information I shared was helpful to you, whether you are an amputee, a caregiver, a family member, or a friend.

Whoever you are, whatever role you're playing in the story, or wherever you are in the story, I hope that this has helped you gain insight, understanding, hope, encouragement, and I hope you laughed a bit… because life is joyful, even if you, or a loved one, has been thrown a curveball.

My hope is that this book will help you get your stance at the plate, keep your eye on that curveball, and knock that sucker out of the park!

L→R: Alyssa, Jim, Jackie, and Michael – after we all successfully completed the 2021 Virginia Mason Mother's Day 5K Walk/Run. Check out those medals!

JAMES R. MOREY

Jim Morey is a Software Engineer, Technology Consultant and a multiple-time #1 Bestselling Author. He is a top-rated Udemy Course Creator and a nationally recognized Book Writing and Publishing Coach.

Jim worked at Microsoft for over 18 years in server and Internet technologies including IIS, Operations Manager, SharePoint, and Azure, has written over 250K lines of code in C#, VB, javaScript, PowerShell, and has worked heavily in HTML5, CSS, T-SQL. Over the last seven years, he created several end-to-end marketing platforms.

Aside from these, he has also focused his humor and resources to overcome the challenges of a below the knee amputation and also help others overcome these challenges.

Jim thoroughly enjoys traveling, bicycle riding, cooking, savoring delicious food from many different cultures, and is on a Keto-lifestyle. Most of all, he's a blessed Husband and a proud Dad of their two kids.

CHAPTER 8
FEARLESS TO SOAR AND SHINE
By Mildred Borbon Osias

Arise, shine, for your light has come, and the glory of the LORD rises upon you.

Isaiah 60:1 NIV

Fear is paralyzing. It binds our hands and feet to muzzle us into inability. It traps us in the room of its genesis. We deflate under the weight of panic and anxiety.

Ironically, the only vivid memory of my generally happy toddler years was a three-inch spider crawling up my arm. The picture is scorched in high-density inside my head. My fear of spiders has long been trounced, but the birthplace of fear was never forgotten. It takes faith to recast the prison of cowardice to a preface of courage.

One of our most incapacitating fears is the fear of exuding our bright radiance from God. Jesus is the light of the world, and He shines His light through us. We are the salt and light of the earth. We preserve and illuminate the world through the grace and character of our Savior. When we are liberated from fear, we can soar and bring God's light as high as we can to brighten the lives of our family, friends, city, nation and the world.

The verse in Isaiah 60:1 was a declaration of victory for Israel. In the previous chapters, the prophet described the gloom and doom of darkness surrounding the nation because they failed to uphold their faith. They allowed other people to overshadow their righteousness.

Darkness induces us to lie down, sleep and be lethargic. But as the morning dawns, the light compels us to arise, awaken and bustle. Isaiah told Israel that "the Light" has come. God is light, and He has emancipated us from darkness to soar and shine.

It is, therefore, heartbreaking that many Christians recoil from their purpose. We cower in fear from displaying the transformational power of God. We have the gift to heal the sick, but we rarely pray in faith for the sick. We can redeem people from darkness, yet we shrink back from sharing the good news of Jesus' saving grace. We can change the atmosphere around us, but we choose to wallow in our sorrows, struggles, and challenges. We hardly utilize the limitless reservoir of resources to bring freedom to people's lives. We even compromise our values to ease our pain, humiliation or struggles, instead of entrusting our lives to God.

Edmund Burke, a British statesman, said, "The only thing necessary for the triumph of evil is for good men to do nothing." As Christians, we do not have the right to think small of our existence because we carry the light that brings hope. We have a huge responsibility to cast that light on the world. We are carriers of God's presence. If not for godly character, the world would be in anarchy and despair.

If the moon were unable to reflect the light of the sun, our nights would not have been so lovely. Many songs and stories about the beauty of the light of the moon would not have been written. Though it may not be a light as bright as the sun, its significance is not meaningful.

If beacons fail to beam, many ocean vessels would be lost and shipwrecked. What would the night be if we did not have candles and light bulbs? How would the world be without all these sources of light like fire and lasers?

Our light is extinguished by our lack of confidence in God's light in us. We fear demonstrating the power of God because people who shine are lashed. They are either criticized or reckoned as arrogant. The world's envy toward those who are great makes us fearful of excelling in our gifts and soaring high.

We mistakenly think that it is better to blend in with the crowd because our victories would bring unnecessary attention. The eyes that follow us create the fear that we could not sustain our accomplishments.

People empathize more with mistakes and shortcomings. We feel akin to failures and misery. It seems that those who show much of their flaw are more commended for being "a real human."

Sadly, we feel more gratification in our frailty than in our might. How ignorant are we, living in oblivion, that the reason we see clearly is because of the light that righteous people have shone in front of us. Their light is the reason we move forward and aim for something better.

As Christians, we have a more noble cause to shine. We glorify God through the righteousness and victories that people see in us.

We get excited with movies depicting success. We applaud those who took the courage to be prominent. We celebrate champions, and yet we are fearful of being in their position.

We are terrified of haters, disapproval and rejection. We fear the rage of envy. Pressures tear us.

We are scared to fail.

Hence, we become blind to those whose lives were touched and changed by human triumphs.

SOAR AND SHINE IN EXCELLENCE

Mediocrity should be considered a sin because it does not employ faith. The parable of the servants who were given talents in Matthew 25 provides us with a hint that excellence is a necessary virtue in the Kingdom of God.

I am not talking about simply being a world champion in sports, education, science or arts. If we can, why not? We can own the stages of the world to proclaim God. But if we should excel, let us excel first and foremost in our faith.

I know that I sound like an idealist when I talk about soaring and shining. But I firmly believe every word in the Bible. I fully trust in the power of God.

Yes, I have witnessed the weakness of man. I, myself, have my fair share of failures and faults. But I refuse to accept that my limitations are the standard of my life.

My God is bigger than anything.

Nothing should stop us from moving forward and being triumphant, no matter how many times we have stumbled because God promised to transform us from glory to glory.

Joshua 1:7 NIV
Be strong and very courageous. Be careful to obey all the law my servant Moses gave you; do not turn from it to the right or to the left, that you may be successful wherever you go.

I once asked my husband, Raymond, if he ever felt tired, discouraged or regretful choosing to serve in ministry. He said that since he gave his life to God, he trusted Him wholly, and there was no room for negative emotions. No wonder he was called to be a pastor. He was easily contented with God and rarely disappointed. I had never seen him bitter toward anyone, even when he had the right to be angry and hurt.

For more than 35 years, he had the most attendance in prayer meetings. He would only miss it when he was ill or had an emergency – about twice or thrice in a year. He never missed Sunday worship. During vacation, we attend or preach somewhere or watch online. He is a work-in-progress like all of us, but he has allowed God to progress His life considerably.

Amid the controversies among famous Christian leaders, I thank God for the people around us who remind us that God's grace and power are real. Very few Christians have this stubborn constancy in righteousness, but their brilliance is comforting.

2 Corinthians 8:7 NIV
But since you excel in everything – in faith, in speech, in knowledge, in complete earnestness and in the love we have kindled in you – see that you also excel in this grace of giving.

The Bible clearly tells us to excel in everything. Excellence does not mean that you must beat records and be a recognized champion. Instead, it means that you keep trying to reach your full potential. Your standard is not the appraisal of the world but the approval of God.

SOAR LIKE AN EAGLE

Isaiah 40:31 NIV
But those who hope in the LORD will renew their strength. They will soar on wings like eagles; they will run and not grow weary; they will walk and not be faint.

For years I have been fascinated by this Biblical analogy that I have researched a lot on eagles[19]. Because they are huge and beautiful, simply their presence is intimidating to little birds that develop the Napoleon complex. The small birds start feeling insecure, and without cause, they gang up and begin to heckle and peck eagles. In short, eagles are bullied most of their lives just for looking gorgeous and being powerful.

Crows would sometimes perch on an eagle's back to peck him. But instead of fighting back, the eagle simply spreads its wings and soars upward. The higher the eagle goes, the more difficult it is for crows to attack. The crows quickly lose oxygen and pass out as eagles speed up their flight to 160

---
[19] Facts.net. Eagle Facts. https://facts.net/nature/animals/eagle-facts

kilometers per hour to reach high altitudes of about 15,000 feet.

Eagles get excited when storms come. That is because they can ride on the storm's wind and soar for days gliding on its power without flapping their wings. They fly higher with significantly less effort. The eagles, having the longest wingspan among birds and can glide for days without a break. God is the "wind beneath our wings."

How interesting that God inspired the prophet Isaiah to use this analogy for those who trust in Him. The higher we soar with God, the lesser we are bothered by the little things that weigh down our lives. Instead of wasting our time perturbed by insignificant issues, let us focus on excelling in our calling.

Immigrating to Europe was a test of trust to soar with God.

It was an intimidating place when my family first came to Denmark as missionaries on November 4, 1998. There were so many hurdles, but we leaped through each of them because we were confident of our calling.

We befriended people in buses, parties and events to share the gospel. We were only armed with faith and vision – to have a community church in every major city of Europe. Things were tough, but as we soared higher with God, He graced us with success.

From Copenhagen, we pioneered our first daughter church in Oslo, Norway, in 2005. Then came the other churches.

Who would have thought that now we have daughter churches and granddaughter churches in Madrid, Athens, Paris, Barcelona, Helsinki, Sandvika, Oslo West, Netherlands,

General Santos and sister churches in Zurich and Saint Gallen?

All these churches have a tremendous passion for discipleship as they were raised in the faith. The remarkable thing is, *educated missionaries* did not pioneer them. Almost all these churches were started by au pairs, who came to know the Lord through FCC (Filadelfia Christian Church). They were trained through our local discipleship programs during their two-year visa.

There are no ordinary Christians with an extraordinary God. Nothing can stop us from soaring whenever we move with God.

LIGHT SAVIOR

Matthew 5:14-16 NIV
"You are the light of the world. A town built on a hill cannot be hidden. Neither do people light a lamp and put it under a bowl. Instead, they put it on its stand, and it gives light to everyone in the house. In the same way, let your light shine before others, that they may see your good deeds and glorify your Father in heaven.

In 2018, our church community, FCC Copenhagen, entitled our camp "*Effulgence*." It sparked so much interest because it was such a big word. The definitions are: a brilliant radiance; a shining forth[20]; the ability to shine brightly, and the state of looking very beautiful or being full of goodness[21]; shining brilliantly; resplendent[22].

---

[20] www.dictionary.com

[21] Cambridge Dictionary

[22] American Heritage Dictionary

FEARLESS TO SOAR AND SHINE

Ephesians 5:8-14 NIV
For you were once darkness, but now you are light in the Lord. Live as children of light (for the fruit of the light consists in all goodness, righteousness and truth) and find out what pleases the Lord. Have nothing to do with the fruitless deeds of darkness, but rather expose them. It is shameful even to mention what the disobedient do in secret. But everything exposed by the light becomes visible — and everything that is illuminated becomes a light. This is why it is said:

"Wake up, sleeper,
rise from the dead,
and Christ will shine on you."

Brushing up on the uses and importance of light brought me to a state of awe toward the Lord as always. Light brings out the beauty of things. When there is light, the true colors of creation come out. Light in itself is beautiful. It is made up of different colors visible to the human eye when it passes through a prism. The most common manifestation of a light spectrum is the rainbow.

Besides its beauty, light is also very useful. It sustains life. Plants produce their food through the sunlight. Ultraviolet light helps humans synthesize vitamin D and enhance mood. Microwaves are used for cooking. Infrared light is employed in pain management and communication. X-rays are essential as a diagnostic tool. Gamma rays treat diseases.

Should we even talk about the importance of lasers? Light gives visibility, communicates, yields energy, promotes healing, disinfects and so on. There are a million functions of light.

As Christians, we are bearers of God's light that sustains life.

Have you ever experienced people being drawn to you for no apparent reason, like a moth to a light? I always wondered why strangers made a beeline to ask for directions from me or ask for help. I look very Asian, so there is a huge possibility that I do not speak the Danish language, and yet I am a magnet for old folks here in Denmark asking for assistance. Do I look kinder than others?

When I was a young, painfully timid Christian, I felt uneasy that people chose to come to me. Through the years, though, I realized that they were attracted to the light – the presence of God through me.

This light is not visible to the naked eye, but it shines brightly in the spiritual realm. Ever since I realized that, I started praying for people who come to me. I invited the old folks I met at the hospital and gave out our church's calling card. They were my motivation to learn Danish and be able to communicate.

We need to make opportunities to radiate God's light wherever.

At a Filipino community event in Denmark, a woman approached me to introduce her teenage children. She was grateful that I had offered help many years ago when she was struggling at the airport with her two small children. I had helped care for the young toddlers throughout the flight – from Denmark to the Philippines. She had been telling people about the act of kindness that was shown to her. Interestingly, I usually only have so much patience for my own children. Grace multiplies the drop of oil we have into jars of blessings.

Light has a long-range influence. Denmark is a prime example. This country has a very high level of integrity. It is the least corrupt nation in the world and was also voted as the number one happiest nation. I believe that they are still reaping the blessings of the faith and obedience of their Christian forefathers. As God promised, those who love Him will be blessed to a thousand generations.

Christians have an enormous responsibility to set the atmosphere of their communities. When we shine for God, people eventually follow that light.

Christians must have a high level of integrity such that they would not need the law to regulate their actions. We call it self-government. Law-abiding citizens should not be forged by the law but molded by internal uprightness.

We should never engage in anything that would hurt God's name. Why would we put ourselves in a position where God cannot bless us? Trusting God brings more abundance than the world could offer.

Even in seemingly mundane things, we maintain our righteousness. Consider the world your home, so keep it clean and safe. Our church has been complimented countless times that we leave the place we used in a state cleaner than when we arrived.

My children were brought up to respect the environment and never throw things on the road. If Europeans clean up their tables after eating in fast-food restaurants, Christians worldwide can do better.

There are limitless opportunities to be a light to the world, whether in integrity, kindness, love, patience and the like. The most important thing is, we should be as bright and functional as light in big and small matters.

A HEALTHY SELF-WORTH

A thin line separates the noble and ignoble. To "soar and shine" does not mean that we become blind to our imperfection. Every person is totally depraved, needing the grace of God. Every Christian is in gradual improvement. If we no longer see or acknowledge our transgression and inadequacy, then we are in self-deception.

In Romans, the apostle Paul said that he was a wretched man who was a slave to a body disposed to death but delivered by Jesus. In the proceeding chapters, Paul talked about the power of God to unshackle us from bondage. He used to be very arrogant, being highly educated and with a high position. But his encounter with Jesus transformed his mind. Paul acknowledged his weakness but exalted the power of God even more. He considered his achievements worth nothing compared to His experience with God, but he did not set his knowledge and wisdom aside. Instead, he developed a healthy self-worth and utilized his past experiences to pursue his purpose in making Jesus known.

I was once asked if Jesus debated and argued. I said that as far as I can remember from my regular Bible readings, He did not. Jesus had intelligent discussions, explanations, answers to questions, and the like, but there was no need to argue because He was confident of who He was. He did not flinch, claiming that He was the "I AM" (God's old testament identity. YHWH)

I follow the same principle; there is no need to prove yourself right when you know that God is your advocate. "Vengeance is mine, I will repay," says the Lord (Romans 12:19 NKJV). He knows what is just and fair; therefore, He tells us not to avenge ourselves. Why should we worry about what people say when God vindicates us or shows favor to us?

Besides being overly defensive, most of us are also plagued with poor self-esteem. I used to have a victim mentality. Everyone was to blame *except me*. It took many years of walking with Jesus to learn to take responsibility for my mistakes and choices.

Moreover, as a Filipina, my poor self-worth was aggravated by cultural values that prevented me from being confident. In the Philippines, we typically feel awkward receiving compliments. It was construed as being proud. A Danish colleague once complimented me, and I said, "Oh, not really." She then asked, "Did you think I was lying or saying flattery?" I was so embarrassed and said that I thought she was just being kind. She said the proper answer to compliments was, "Thank you."

Accepting who God made us is not boasting. It is deep gratitude and appreciation for His goodness and generosity. Gifts and talents were given to encourage, enhance and empower people around us.

We need to see ourselves through the eyes of God and acknowledge who we truly are. We are God's children, beloved and precious to Him. Jesus called us His friends. We have direct access to God through the blood of Jesus. Jesus saved us from death and condemnation. We were appointed as God's ambassadors. We are a royal priesthood. We are the temple of the Holy Spirit. We were fearfully and wonderfully made. We can do all things through Christ who strengthens us. These are just a few of what the Bible tells about us. We become fearless to soar and shine because we know who we are in God.

THE MIND OF A WINNER

2 Corinthians 10:5 NIV
We demolish arguments and every pretension that sets itself up against the knowledge of God, and we take captive every thought to make it obedient to Christ.

Romans 12:1-2 NIV
Therefore, I urge you, brothers and sisters, in view of God's mercy, to offer your bodies as a living sacrifice, holy and pleasing to God---this is your true and proper worship. Do not conform to the pattern of this world but be transformed by the renewing of your mind. Then you will be able to test and approve what God's will is---his good, pleasing and perfect will.

According to the World Health Organization, people living in depression and anxiety increased by 18.4% between 2005 and 2015. This decline in global mental health is quite alarming. The WHO estimates that a total of 27% of the population, 264 million, or 1 in 5 people are depressed[23].

Medical professionals believe that we are nurturing a culture of despair. Gaming and the internet may connect us globally, but it also creates a different kind of isolation. Lesser community and personal interactions have predisposed people to a decreased ability to cope with stress and pressure. Since the standards are set so high in almost every aspect,

---

[23] World Health Organization https://www.who.int/news-room/fact-sheets/detail/depression

success becomes a burden. Even bright children are now underachieving because the spotlight is shone on what people lack instead of celebrating their excellence.

Psychogenic death[24] or give-up-itis is an actual medical condition that has caught many researchers' attention and is being studied more in-depth. In an article found in the National Library of Medicine, it was described as a death induced by extreme emotion, usually fear, when a person loses hope or does not see a way out of his situation. It was first observed in 1942 and then among prisoners of war or those who had been through traumatic experiences. A completely healthy person can die in three days when he becomes utterly hopeless.

To counteract this growing culture of despair, we can promulgate God's way of thinking.

The winner's mind is full of life. It never thinks of itself as a victim but an overcomer.

Fear makes us insecure. Insecurity makes us easily offended, defensive and detached. When our identities are secure in Christ, everything said, and whatever incidents that happen can become constructive criticisms that open our minds and mature our actions. We listen and assess objectively from **faith** and *not* from **fear**.

An insecure mind often ruins our principled actions, good intentions, and it kills hope. We worry about what other people might think or say.

---

[24] National Library of Medicine. https://pubmed.ncbi.nlm.nih.gov/494838

Here are some examples: *"If I volunteer, they might think I am ostentatious." "If I give more than the others, they might think I am bragging." "If I do this ... they might think that."* We put thoughts in people's minds before they even think about it.

Let us take on the winner's mind that is set on the finish line. The winner does not worry about what the audience would say. He trained for the race and is set on finishing it.

Isaiah 26:3
You will keep in perfect peace all who trust in you, all whose thoughts are fixed on you!

Proverbs 23:7 NKJV
For as he thinks in his heart, so is he."

I have been reading up on coaching principles and was reminded of the Zeigarnik and Ovsiankina effect[25]. Zeigarnik postulates that we remember with clarity and intensity unfinished business in our lives. In short, unless there is a closure, it is hard to move on. Ovsiankina, her colleague, expanded on this. She observed that people try to take up and finish those that have not been concluded. It is a relevant analogy that sometimes the struggles and challenges we have, stay with us and continue to gnaw and eat us up because we have not resolved them in our hearts and minds.

Romans 12:1-2 states that renewing the mind is a powerful tool to close the past doors. A bad habit can only be stopped if it is replaced by a good one. When we focus our mind on a better thing, our mind develops new neural pathways to

---

[25] http://www.soulsearching.life/web/pages/soulsearching/The-Zeigarnik-Effect-ways-to-Improve-Motivation-and-Memory.aspx

overwrite the old mentality and learn new positive cognitive skills.

As always, the Bible is so supreme that modern science simply validates the truth it has revealed since ancient times. Moreover, it uses language that is so simple and understandable. Humans only complicate it by doubt and fear. Once we accept God's principles, our lives get simplified again. Closure does not come with time. It happens when we finally embrace grace and forgiveness.

Philippians 4:6-8 NIV
Do not be anxious about anything, but in every situation, by prayer and petition, with thanksgiving, present your requests to God. And the peace of God, which transcends all understanding, will guard your hearts and your minds in Christ Jesus. Finally, brothers and sisters, whatever is true, whatever is noble, whatever is right, whatever is pure, whatever is lovely, whatever is admirable---if anything is excellent or praiseworthy---think about such things.

The winner's mind does not dwell on pain. Countless times I have heard of athletes who endured excruciating pain to get to where they wanted to be.

The wounded heart is filled with fear. It does not trust. It is suspicious. Hence, it cannot move forward. It cannot soar high. It is stuck in a dark place with no windows or doors.

"Do not get hurt. If you get hurt, the ones we are saving will lose their lives." Yoo Shi-Jin: Descendants of the Sun (Korean drama series)

It was a command from the officer-in-charge. In the mini-series, it was an instruction given to the soldiers. It referred to all - physical, emotional and mental states. They had to make sure that they were vigorous enough to rescue people who were in danger. In life, it is a command we should take seriously from the Lord.

Proverbs 4:23 NKJV
Keep your heart with all diligence, for out of it spring the issues of life.

Decisions made at the height of emotions bring so much regret. We could miss the most remarkable things in our life when we allow a history of pain to rule us. Words said in anger can destroy the sweetest of relationships. Fear can lead us to dishonor the Lord in the most painful way.

As a church leader, staying hurt compromises our mission to save souls. God's preventive measure is to put our faith in His everlasting love.

1 Peter 5:7 NLT
"Give all your worries and cares to God, for he cares about you."

A book I once read said, "Jesus refused to be offended ... hence, he remained sinless.[26]" I love that. I believe we have the power to choose our responses and take charge of our emotions. Jesus procured that on the cross for us. True freedom is the liberty to do what is right.

I say this over and over to my mentees and Lifegroup. "Your first reaction reveals who you really are. Your second reaction reveals who you choose to be." The devil always plays our emotions. He knows that hurt impairs our judgment, makes us impulsive, damages relationships, escalates our pride,

---

[26] When Heaven Invades Earth. Bill Johnson. Destiny Image Publishers. 2013. Chapter 2

forces us to abandon our calling, deviates us from our extraordinary destiny and weakens the church.

Nursed hurt becomes bitterness that gives birth to several kinds of dangerous sins. The saddest effect is that we miss helping many people come to know Jesus as their Lord and Savior. Staying hurt brings not only our death but the sure death of others. Praise God His love and grace heal the deepest pain and restore the most wretched and afflicted heart.

God's presence is the balm that heals and makes us recover. Bring your crushed heart to God, so He can pulverize it further and destroy every piece of hurt; then, He will re-shape it into a healthy one - ready to love, forgive and trust again. This is a habit we need to develop for rapid recovery.

The winner's mind is forever learning and forever coping. No matter how much we know in any area, there are always new things to learn and things we have previously learned that we need to refresh. We put on the humility to learn from everyone. There are times when God leaves huge question marks as tools in our lives to stretch our faith.

Hebrews 5:8 NLT
Even though Jesus was God's Son, he learned obedience from the things he suffered.

THE STABLE LIGHT OF PERFECT PEACE

Peace is like a reliable, steady light. I get entranced with emergency lights – the ones that are always on or turn on when the main electric power shuts down. I see peace as an emergency light that never goes off. It might not be shining all the time, but it will always emerge in the most distressing moments.

The remarkable thing about supernatural peace is that it is inexplicable and incomprehensible, but it is there when it is not supposed to be; it is there when circumstances are most challenging. It is there simply because God is there with you. It is so baffling, perplexing, confounding, and mysterious, and yet it feels oh so good.

Peace is a light that exhibits our faith. When everyone panics and worries, they, too, could calm down by simply observing our state of confidence and peace. It takes a *lot* of courage to be still, to do nothing, and know that God is God. The song "Still" beautifully paints that picture, "I will soar with You above the storm."

It is scary to be the center of attention as one manifests radiance. Some will be annoyed because your light of uprightness will expose their sin and weaknesses. The demons squirm in God's presence. Some will try to pull you down to their level. However, many will be inspired, encouraged to seek Jesus, and be empowered like you.

Fear liberates evil to roam with audacity. Being fearless liberates righteousness to own its territory. What would you liberate?

As we acknowledge that our light emanates from God, arrogance is taken over by humility. We know that we are where we are because of the grace of God. Why would we shrink back from brilliance when we know we are simply reflecting it from God?

Our luster displays the Lord's love and saving power. That is inspiring. That gives hope. That makes others want the presence of God in their lives.

What a fantastic testimony when God is *always* greater than anything we go through. What a sight when our challenges drown in the depth of God's might.

No one is powerful *apart* from God. We are all ridden with failure and vulnerability as human beings. Yet would it not be marvelous that when people look at us, they see God instead of our frailty?

The theme of our lives changed when we invited Jesus to reside in our hearts. Our former vocabulary was filled with words like downtrodden, weak, defeat, struggle, problem and the like. But as soon as the Lord's feet entered the door of our lives, our words were reinvented: joy, strength, victory, overcome, challenge and the like. Our brokenness became battle scars of victory. Our weaknesses became steppingstones to our fortes.

I have often been called an eternal optimist because I seem to consistently see the bright side of life and perceive the good in people in intense yellow highlights. I take this as a compliment.

Those who have known me for many years know this was not who I was before. I was insecure, had very poor self-esteem, easily offended, bitter and very pessimistic.

What changed? Jesus came into my life. As I walked daily with Him, I did not even notice that my character was radically shifting.

For years now, my family and I live in God's unfathomable peace. We want a burden-free life. After thousands of experiences of how God rescued us, how can we even have the right to doubt Him? A common adage said, "Why worry when you can pray?"

On June 28, 2016, our family was at Ataturk airport in Istanbul when three suicide bombers came to wreak havoc!

My sons decided to go to a coffee shop, but my husband and I found a place to rest and charge our phones. I called them back. They reluctantly returned to charge their phones.

Suddenly, while we were doing so, gunshots were fired, and people started running. It was unbelievable how calm we were. We put on our shoes, unplugged our chargers and collected our phones and bags in a few seconds before running to find a safe place.

There were more gunshots and running. Then a bomb blasted, right below the coffee shop where my sons planned to go. I was able to post a short plea for prayer on Facebook. Then I got messages from reporters which I could not respond to.

While running away from the blast, we saw terrified people finding a secure place to hide. We remained composed and alert. At one time, we stopped and prayed together.

I also asked my sons if they sincerely had a personal relationship with God. I told them that they would not go to heaven if they died simply because they have parents who were ministers. In the middle of a terrifying situation, we found time to laugh! My sons assured me that they responded to me sharing the gospel a thousand times since they were babies.

We were in a life-and-death situation, so I had to make sure. We knew that Jesus would definitely appear whichever way the situation ended. I wanted all of us to surely meet God, either in Turkey or in heaven. Sadly, this tragedy took the lives of 41 people and injured 230.

In one area, a teenager had a panic attack, and her mom looked so helpless. I came and asked if I could help and pray for her daughter. The mother agreed. I hugged the teenager and started praying. She began to breathe normally and calmed down.

An Asian woman came to my husband and asked, "How can you be so calm?" She had been running and hiding together with the crowd we were with and saw how we prayed for people. Our answer was simple: We knew God was with us.

The drama and tragedy did not end there.

We were asked to leave the airport and walk through the exit where the bodies, blood and rubble were! We were placed in busses that drove an hour away and were dropped at Taksim square, where we were told to find a place to stay overnight. We found opportunities to help people but lacked the resources to assist even more.

In the morning, the Lord gave us the wisdom to rebook our flight through a friend in Denmark. Otherwise, we would have wasted precious hours lining up at the booking counters.

We said a prayer for those who were hurt and the families of those who lost their lives. Then we decided to see the beautiful city of Istanbul. Most people would probably refrain from going out after that tragic incident, but we knew the Lord was with us. We never regretted that decision because we got to see the beautiful Blue Mosque. We also stopped at

Hagia Sophia, a Christian church, and we prayed for Turkey's salvation.

God orchestrated everything that happened to our family during that fateful time, that it came out as an undying lovely song of triumph.

To this day, that experience is a trophy for the Lord. Years of walking with God made us who we were on that day. **Fearlessness** was not formed in an instant. It was the product of constantly trusting God through many years.

Arise. Shine. For your Light has come.

As I ended writing, the song "Light of a Million Mornings" started playing in my heart.

Taken at the Hagia Sophia, Istanbul, on June 29, 2016
From left: Abdiel Reigh, Andrew Reyhan, Raymond, Mildred,

MILDRED BORBON OSIAS

Mildred Osias has started and co-pastored FCC churches in Europe with her husband, Raymond, since 1998 (www.fccc-family.com).

She was a Registered Nutritionist-Dietician, who graduated from the University of the Philippines (U.P.) in Diliman.

She responded to God's call to full-time ministry in 1987 and finished a second bachelor's degree in Theology at Bethel Bible College. She later went back to U.P. to pursue MBA.

She has a passion for discipleship and has authored most of the discipleship materials used in their churches. She has also been a conference speaker for several years.

Her passion is teaching and discipleship. Her missions experience is quite extensive, from Asia and Europe. She considers being a small group (Lifegroup) leader and mentor, without a break for 36 years, her most significant contribution in ministry.

CHAPTER 9
FEARLESS FAITH
by Rev. Dante Eleazar L. Simon

"Now faith is the assurance of things hoped for, the conviction of things not seen."

Hebrews 11:1 ESV

"Courage is not the absence of fear, but the triumph over it. The brave man is not he who does not feel afraid, but he who conquers that fear."

– Nelson Mandela

Before we discuss what "Fearless Faith" means, what does the word "fearless" mean in the first place?

"Fearless" is dictionary-defined as being bold, brave, dauntless, courageous, and to be free from fear.

One of my favorite scriptures when circumstances, relationship issues or other challenges tempt me to become fearful is Psalm 121:1-2 ESV *"I lift up my eyes to the hills. From where does my help come? My help comes from the Lord, who made heaven and earth."*

Another quote that has helped me to face daunting situations is from Robert Fanny who said: *"Courage is not the absence of fear or despair; it is the capacity to continue on despite them, no matter how great or overwhelming they become."*

And a poem by Antonio Machado – who is considered one of the greatest Spanish poets of the 20th century – has impacted my life:

Traveler, your footprints are the only road, nothing else. Traveler, there is no road; you make your own path as you walk. As you walk, you make your own road, and when you look back you see the path you will never travel again. Traveler, there is no road; only a ship's wake on the sea.

One of the most potent forces against *fear* is this supernatural power called *faith*, the kind of faith that's been tested through trials and tribulations, and a faith that's unshakeable.

To me, faith *can* and *will* overcome fear.

It is one of the ultimate opposing forces against fear, and this is why I've entitled this chapter "Fearless Faith."

a. Hebrews 11:3 NIV states: *"By faith we understand that the universe was formed at God's command, so that what is seen was not made out of what was visible."* This happened when God simply commanded, *"Let there be light."* [Genesis 1:3]

As the Psalmist explained: *By the word of the LORD the heavens were made, and all the host of them by the breath of His mouth... For He spoke, and it was done; He commanded, and it stood fast."* [Psalm 33:6, 9]

b. By *faith* we understand. We did not see this act of creation; we only know of it **by faith**. We also know this by *reason*, because we know the world was created and created by an intelligent Designer. Again, this is faith going *beyond,* and yet **not** in *contradiction* to reason.

Even in times when it seems that God expects a faith that contradicts reason, closer examination reveals He does not.

For example, it might seem contrary to reason for God to expect Abraham to believe that Sarah's dead womb could bring forth a child. But it is ***not unreasonable*** to believe that the God who created life and the womb could do this, and that He would do it according to His promise.

By faith we understand: This text *does not* say that God created the world *with* or *by* faith. Since God sees and knows all things, "faith" in a human sense does not apply to Him. Since we understand faith as *the substance of things hoped for, the evidence of things not seen*, what know that God sees everything and does not "hope" for anything.

So, things which are seen in our physical world were not made of things which are visible. At the time the Book of Hebrews was written, most scientists believed the universe was created out of *existing matter*, **not** out of nothing. They believed the world was made out of things which were visible.

But the Bible corrects this misunderstanding, clearly stating that the world was not made of things which are visible.

Faith at the beginning of man's history

Abel's faith

Hebrews 11:4 NKJV states: *"By faith Abel offered to God a more excellent sacrifice than Cain, through which he obtained witness that he was righteous, God testifying of his gifts; and through it he being dead still speaks."*

a. Looking at this part of the scripture: "By faith Abel offered to God a more excellent sacrifice" – we see that the difference between the sacrifice of Cain and the sacrifice of Abel in Genesis 4:3-5 was not between the superiority of an animal sacrifice (firstborn lambs) vs. crops (fruits of the ground). The difference was that Abel's sacrifice was made ***by faith***.

b. As Calvin conveyed: *"Abel's sacrifice was preferred to his brother's for no other reason than that it was sanctified by faith; for surely the fat of brute animals did not smell so sweetly, that it could, by its odor, pacify God."*

c. God testifying of his gifts: It is likely that God testified of His pleasure with Abel's sacrifice by consuming it with fire from heaven, as happened at the dedication of the tabernacle in Leviticus 9:24, the temple in 2 Chronicles 7:1, and upon offerings made by David in 1 Chronicles 21:26 and Elijah in 1 Kings 18:38.

Let's note that the writer to the Hebrews didn't say that it is *difficult* to please God without faith. He said that it is impossible.

American Bible teacher and pastor Newell points out: *"These two elements seem most simple, but, alas, how many professing*

Christians act as if God were not living; and how many others, though seeking after Him, are not expecting from Him as Rewarder!"

Noah's faith

Let's look at the faith of Noah.

Hebrews 11: 7 NKJV states: *"By faith Noah, being divinely warned of things not yet seen, moved with godly fear, prepared an ark for the saving of his household, by which he condemned the world and became heir of the righteousness which is according to faith."*

Noah was divinely warned of things not yet seen. God warned Noah of a coming flood – something that had never happened before in the history of the world.

His faith was demonstrated in not merely agreeing that the flood would come, but in doing what God told him to do regarding the flood – he built an ark because he was moved with godly fear.

Noah prepared for and built an ark, which took him *decades* to complete.

Real faith will always *do* something. The book of James repeats this theme over and over again.

By his actions, Noah *condemned* the world.

We shouldn't think that Noah was a man who preached sermons of condemnation to the world. Instead, his mere conduct, his faith in action, without any preaching at all, could feel like condemnation to the world.

Faith in the Life of Abraham and the Patriarchs

Abraham's obedience by faith

Now let's look at Abraham's faith.

Hebrews 11:8 NKJV: *"By faith Abraham obeyed when he was called to go out to the place which he would receive as an inheritance. And he went out, not knowing where he was going."*

Abraham obeyed by **faith**.

He stepped out in faith, going to the place God promised him; but his faith was less than perfect.

This is seen by comparing Genesis 12:1-5 with Acts 7:2-4, where it is evident that Abraham first went half way to where God called him, and then only *eventually* did he obey completely.

Yet thousands of years later, God incredibly chose not to "remember" Abraham's delayed obedience; HE only affirmed Abraham's faith.

Abraham's sojourning life of faith

By faith Abraham sojourned in the Promised land as *in* a foreign country.

In other words, instead of building houses, he dwelt in tents with Isaac and Jacob, who were his heirs of the same promise because Abraham looked forward into the future, and waited for the city whose builder and maker *is* God.

Verses That Help us to Be Courageous in our Faith

Psalm 27:1-3 ESV *"The Lord is my light and my salvation; whom shall I fear? The Lord is the stronghold of my life; of whom shall I be afraid? When evildoers assail me to eat up my flesh, my adversaries and foes, it is they who stumble and fall. Though an army encamp against me, my heart shall not fear; though war arise against me, yet I will be confident."*

Matthew 10:26 ESV *"So have no fear of them, for nothing is covered that will not be revealed, or hidden that will not be known."*

Luke 12:22-26 ESV *"And he said to his disciples, "Therefore I tell you, do not be anxious about your life, what you will eat, nor about your body, what you will put on. For life is more than food, and the body more than clothing. Consider the ravens: they neither sow nor reap, they have neither storehouse nor barn, and yet God feeds them. Of how much more value are you than the birds! And which of you by being anxious can add a single hour to his span of life? If then you are not able to do as small a thing as that, why are you anxious about the rest?"*

Isaiah 43:1 ESV *"But now thus says the Lord, he who created you, O Jacob, he who formed you, O Israel: 'Fear not, for I have redeemed you; I have called you by name, you are mine.'"*

Psalm 91:1-5 ESV *"He who dwells in the shelter of the Most High will abide in the shadow of the Almighty. I will say to the Lord, "My refuge and my fortress, my God, in whom I trust." For he will deliver you from the snare of the fowler and from the deadly pestilence. He will cover you with his pinions, and under his wings you will find refuge; his faithfulness is a shield and buckler. You will not fear the terror of the night, nor the arrow that flies by day..."*

Other Idioms on Courage and Being Fearless

"Courage is rightly esteemed the first of human qualities…because it is the quality which guarantees all others." – Winston Churchill

"Courage is doing what you're afraid to do. There can be no courage unless you're scared." – Eddie Rickenbacker

"Courage is going from failure to failure without losing enthusiasm."

– Winston Churchill

"Courage is not simply one of the virtues but the form of every virtue at the testing point, which means at the point of highest reality." – C.S. Lewis

"There is no living thing that is not afraid when it faces danger. The true courage is in facing danger when you are afraid, and that kind of courage you have in plenty."

– L. Frank Baum, *The Wonderful Wizard of Oz*

"Courage is grace under pressure." – Ernest Hemingway

"Courage doesn't happen when you have all the answers. It happens when you are ready to face the questions you have been avoiding your whole life."

– Shannon L. Adler

"Courage isn't having the strength to go on – it is going on when you don't have strength." – Napoleon Bonaparte

"Courage is resistance to fear, mastery of fear – not absence of fear."

– Mark Twain

"Courage is the first of human qualities because it is the quality which guarantees the others." - Aristotle

5 Verses to Help Us to Become Fearless and to Stay Fearless

Hebrews 11:1 ESV *"Now faith is the assurance of things hoped for, the conviction of things not seen."*

Isaiah 26:3 ESV *"You keep him in perfect peace whose mind is stayed on You, because he trusts in You."*

1 Thessalonians 5:17 ESV *"Pray without ceasing…"*

Matthew 10:28 ESV *"And do not fear those who kill the body but cannot kill the soul. Rather fear him who can destroy both soul and body in hell."*

Psalm 27:1-3 ESV *"The Lord is my light and my salvation; whom shall I fear? The Lord is the stronghold of my life; of whom shall I be afraid? When evildoers assail me to eat up my flesh, my adversaries and foes, it is they who stumble and fall. Though an army encamp against me, my heart shall not fear; though war arise against me, yet I will be confident."*

Action Points That Will Move You Toward Becoming Fearless

I would like to share some important highlights of stories of courageous and fearless faith from the bestselling book *"If You Want to Walk on Water, You Must Get off the Boat"* by John Ortberg.

I've used excerpts from the book and also used my own examples of situations and hindrances you may face that could block you from fulfilling your full potential.

1. Reflect on your own sinful patterns of behavior that have never gotten confronted, move towards and experience transformation.

I invite you to read St. Augustine's biography as an example of someone who experienced true transformation from years of sinful behavior and destructive patterns.

2. Think about your own uncultivated abilities and unused gifts.

Have you heard of the parable of three servants, one who did not use his talent whatsoever, but dug deep in the ground and hid it instead?

The two other servants found success and fulfillment as they invested their talents and harvested double their master's original investments. These were the servants who were willing to explore, cultivate, and even take risks with their talents. The last servant did not only bury his talent, but he even blamed the giver of the gift. So the owner said, "What little you have, will be taken from you and given to the other."

3. Start having deep, honest Conversations you've never had before.

Dr. Anton Boisen came from a family of educators. His forebears were pioneers in a university in the Midwest.

Having trained as a forester, he went on to study theology and philosophy.

Three times he had severe bouts of depression, and had to be confined. Three times he was able to process his illness and came out of the hospital. The events that led him to depression were the death of his mother, unrequited love, severe self pity. He discovered that at the heart of emotional distress was a deep spiritual crisis. He also observed other mental patients and how the Christians ministered to them clinically.

In the 1920s this was unheard of. He was the first to observe and gather a group of 5 seminarians to talk about self-care and psychotherapy. Later he would develop the technique called Clinical Pastoral Approach which would lead to Chaplaincy. Until Boisen had the honest conversations with God and himself, we would never have the modern version of chaplaincy which is self-talk and processing conversations with others usually starting with: Tell me more.

4. Decide to pray great, bold prayers you've never prayed before.

The Prayer of Jabez taken from 1 Chronicles 4:9-10 was turned into a book by Bruce Wilkinson, which sold over nine million copies and became a New York Times bestseller.

"Jabez was more honorable than his brothers. His mother had named him Jabez, saying, "I gave birth to him in pain." Jabez cried out to the God of Israel, saying, "Oh that you would bless me indeed and enlarge my territory! Let your hand be with me, and keep me from

the evil one." And God granted his request." 1 Chronicles 4:9-10 NIV

In the book, Wilkinson encourages Christians to invoke this prayer for themselves on a daily basis.

I invite you to make the Jabez prayer for blessing part of the daily fabric of your life.

5. Make a list of exhilarating risks you never took that you're committed to doing.

I would like to share experiences from my years of ministry in the parish.

In 1999, I pastored a Filipino church in Oakland, California. It was beginning to be clear to the leadership and myself that we needed to move to the tri-city of Union City, Fremont and Hayward to be more missional and reach out to our demographics.

So we negotiated with my District Superintendent and with other neighboring churches, but "we found no room at the inn" and encountered all sorts of excuses regarding why they could not accommodate a fellow Methodist congregation, seeking to share facilities.

Finally, when we were about to give up hope, Wesley Methodist Church in Hayward, California opened their doors to us! Today, we have a vibrant multicultural community of believers in Hayward, California – thanks to the people of Wesley UMC, their beloved pastor Rev. Williamson, and my District Supervisor Dr. Bruce McSpadden. I deeply appreciate their risk-taking ministry.

6. Think about sacrificial services you never offered, that you want to be held accountable to actually doing.

My favorite example is the great missionary Hudson Taylor.

This man of God was called to open the ministry in mainland China. He was a faithful man of God. But the time came when the mission society told him he had to come home because there were no more funds for the missionary work.

At that time he was already making breakthrough in his work. He was given a deadline to pack up his things and leave. The missionary prayed and fasted. And the Lord said to him, "Stay."

Not knowing where his support for his family and ministry would come from, Hudson Taylor was quoted: "If we do God's work God's way, we will never lack God's supply." Indeed, God honored his faithful servant with consistent provision.

7. Reflect on the many lives you never touched that you want to intentionally create time on your calendar to begin connecting.

Bishop Robert Schnase mentioned 3 things that we could do to share God's love and touch peoples lives as persons and congregations.

Risk-Taking Mission and Extravagant Generosity – In 2017 my wife and I decided to follow my brother and mother in Florida to start new ministry in chaplaincy. Fiji missions contacted me to help those new immigrants in the US and missions in the Fiji islands. I gave away everything and I felt I followed Jesus' words: Go sell everything, give to the poor and follow me. Left only with our Corolla and clothes, we journeyed to a place where we had not been before only believing that God was already there.

Intentional Faith development – discipling someone can be the most satisfying thing you can do. Begin to pray for some one whom you could share your faith with and someone you can disciple as one grows deeper in faith in God.

Radical Hospitality – The parsonage has always been a place for people in transit along faiths journey. People have stayed with us from one week to one month to one year. Sometimes becoming a burden, I'll be honest, but becomes joy knowing that one day I will also be a traveler and there will friends along the way.

8. Share with a loved one or close friend some forgotten dreams you'd like to begin working towards.

Happy and blessed are those who dream dreams and are willing to pay the price to make their dreams come true.

Nothing happens unless we dream.

Remember: Today is the first day of the rest of your life.

Don't be afraid to dream, and when you do, dream BIG.

9. Seek after the great God, Who is calling you to be part of something bigger than yourself.

You'll realize there is a world of desperate need, you see the person you can become.

Have you been in a place in your life where you were asking "What if…?"
What if I followed God to become a pastor?
What if I had waited for God's best for me?
What if I enrolled for my MBA?
What if I accepted the new role in a new country?

The common thread to all these *what ifs* is that you will never know what would've happened.

And so, dear Reader, if you want to walk on water, you need to get off the boat.

10. Let this not be your regret on your death bed: You never followed your calling, you never got off the boat.

I celebrate people in my life who have shown me that it is possible to get off the boat and start exploring and living your dream. This is my list of people who got off the boat and used their **fearless faith** to begin to live a courageous life.

Christine Lorenzana Bello – graduated major in Hotel Restaurant Management and Economics – University of the Philippines, worked at Armed Forces of the Philippines, Racks Philippines, Shangrila Asia, LA Rose Restaurant Hollywood, 16 year Veteran, Senior Banker US Bank Global Bank

Maria Amifaith Fider-Reyes – Presiding Judge, Republic of the Philippines, Civic leader, bestselling author

Leni Hufana Del Prado – award-winning writer, actress, model, Christian writer

Arnel de Pano – international singer, composer, choral conductor, award-winning composer, music director, Maestro

Noelle Riza delos Reyes Castillo – Attorney at law, Christian leader, Space Agency of the Philippines, Haggai International, public speaker

Elzar "Dodjie" Simon – Industrial engineer, IT expert, global IT, bestselling author Christian composer and speaker

Rowena Arrieta – world class pianist, Russia's Tchaikovsky laureate in Piano, the only Filipina who holds that distinction

Floy Quintos – award-winning director, actor, stage director, artistic director

Jomar Fleras – playwright, entrepreneur, CEO of Rise Against Hunger, Actor, stage director, business owner

Jackie Lansangan Morey – Jackie is a premier entrepreneur, 9-time #1 International bestselling author, book publisher, consultant, prophetic mentor, WebTV host and Founder of Customer Strategy Academy.

Rev. Dr. Neil Platon – Doctor in Ministry, Claremont Graduate School in Theology, Congregational and Community specialist

Rev. Alex Cambe – leader, California Nevada Conference Conference Committee on Filipino American Ministry, Congregational and Community specialist, Pastor of Grace United Methodist Church - San Francisco Bay area

Rev. Alfredo Casanova – Minister at the United Church of Christ in the Philippines, Congregational and Community organizer

Rev. Dr. Nolf Nolasco, ThD. – Boston University School of Theology, Fuller Seminary, MDiv. Degree in Communications with Honors from the University of the Philippines

Rev. Johann Osias – Congregational and Spiritual Leader, United Methodist Church, Pastor, Servant at St. Paul's UMC, Fremont CA

Vivelyn Pascual – Soprano, University of the Philippines College of Music, Philippine Madrigal Singers, HR Manager at VCP Intermed Philippines, Marketing Chowking, Seafood City USA

My colleagues, the Management and staff Nurses MSW CNAs, Bereavement Coordinator, Volunteer Coordinator, Music Therapist from Promedica Heartland who have shown me what it means to be fearless and courageous in the pandemic situation

My colleagues from Union Seminary who have shown what it means to be a pastor and prophet in the midst of oppression and violence in the Philippines

My high school classmates / batchmates from UPIS 1979 – the best batch ever, who at an early age taught me how to survive and still be fearless and courageous among the best of the best.

Bonus Story: The Tragedy of the Unopened Gift

A story is told of a man who went to heaven and finally met the Lord face to face. The Lord gave him a tour of what was there. He found a small room, almost empty and asked, "What is this room and why are the gifts almost gone?"

The Lord replied, *"Oh, this is the room where people asked for everyday little things that is why it is almost empty. Once we receive the payer request, it is processed and delivered as soon as possible."*

Then the Lord brought him to a super huge place, bigger than an Amazon warehouse where huge boxes, packages and gifts were still undelivered. The man asked Jesus, *"What about these gifts and packages ? Why are they not delivered and opened?"*

"These," the Lord said, *"were the gifts I had planned and were ready for delivery but the saints never asked for them. They forgot that I said: Ask and it shall be given. They are still there until they ask for it. But mostly, they only ask for the small gifts."* How big is your God?

I am who I am by the grace of God. Nothing is an accident with God. He knows what He is doing and He who began a good work will finish it. Don't fear. Even challenges and hardships become building blocks as God executes His plan for us. He wants us to fully develop as humble disciples, fully obedient to His will to make disciples for Christ to transform the world.

I end with a prayer attributed to St Patrick.

"I arise today through God's strength to pilot me, God's might to uphold me, God's wisdom to guide me. God's eye to look before me, Christ's ear to hear me, God's word to speak for me. Christ with me, Christ before me Christ behind me Christ in me, Christ in the heart of everyone who thinks of me Christ beneath me. I arise today In the mighty strength of God."

Praise God.

Standing L→R: Dante Jr., David and Stephen. Front: Pastor Eleazar "Bong" and wife Vivelyn

REV. DANTE ELEAZAR "BONG" SIMON

 Rev. Dante "Bong" Simon is an Ordained United Methodist minister. Having been trained in the Philippines and the United States he has pastored churches from 50 to 500 members in the last 35 years.

Presently he is Spiritual Care Director of Promedica Heartland for Northern California.

He loves singing, drawing, writing poems, gardening and storytelling. Rev. Simon is blessed and happily married to Vivelyn Pascual and blessed with 3 wonderful sons David, Stephen and Dante, Jr.

AFTERWORD

Be not afraid… I go before you. Isaiah 41:10

After reading the stories of all of the writers, I sensed the presence of a faith larger than each of them, which, sustains each of them, as they pursue the goals for each moment in their lives.

For most of them, they wrote about their Christian faith and their belief in the Almighty God who never failed to sustain them.

For some, it is the story of courage despite the challenges of the times.

Overcoming all the voices that wanted to stop them, all the writers in this book, Gemma and Noel Borbon, Leslie Bower, Kenneth Jao, Maria Theresa Trono-Legiralde, Jackie Lansangan-Morey and James Morey, Mildred Osias, Rev. Dante Eleazar Simon, came to the edge, pushed, and flew.

Gemma Borbon wrote about the fear of change, in one's state of health and in one's body. Sometimes, we would not even be able to recognize ourselves, as Gemma Borbon had said it. We would miss "the real me."

Noel Borbon vividly recalled the haunting feeling of fear. He likened it to standing in a dark strange room, at 10 degrees C, uncertain of what could be behind the curtain before it is drawn.

Leslie Bower shared how illness may also foment fear. And yet, this may be used as an occasion by God to call us back to his fold. He is the "Maker" of our time, the "Author" of our life. This is what Leslie Bower shared with us.

Kenneth Jao detailed the business scenario in the Philippines, after the start of the CoVid 19 pandemic. It is the perspective of a man who is constantly weighing his personal interest at stake against keeping his business viable and to provide livelihood for his employees.

Maria Theresa Trono-Legiralde gave a joyful narrative of how courage begins from the simplest things in childhood, all the way to adulthood, and becomes the foundation of grace.

Jackie Morey's chapter gave the reader a guide to help identify one's fears. Jackie lists the different types of fears. More importantly, she gave important action points on how to conquer these fears with practical exercises.

James Morey's chapter is the amazing story of a personal experience and how he conquered fear. It takes a brave heart to read it just as it must have been to write it.

Mildred Borbon Osias made us see how her profound relationship with God has given her a supernatural outlook in life and in coping with fear.

I thank the authors for opening their hearts and taking the time to share their stories.

Anyone who has experienced fear knows how real it is and how limiting it can be. It is not enough to close one's eyes or to remove the cause of fear.

One must see fear in the light of its purpose and meaning in one's life. It may be just a challenge, and therefore a source of gaining virtue. Or it may be a path to sanctity, and therefore a cross that one must embrace.

I close the book happy and content. Fear is a distant memory. I believe I can fly.

Judge Maria Amifaith S. Fider-Reyes

Presiding Judge of the Regional Trial Court (RTC)-Third Judicial Region, Branch 42, City of San Fernando Pampanga; and former Presiding Judge of the RTC-National Capital Judicial Region (NCJR) in Branch 51 Manila, Branch 147 and Branch 61 in Makati City, and Branch 99 in Quezon City, in the Republic of the Philippines.

#1 International Bestselling Author

PLEASE RATE OUR BOOK

My Collaborative-Authors and I would be honored if you would please take a few moments to rate our book on Amazon.com (U.S.).

Or, if you're in any of these countries, please use these Amazon sites:

Amazon.ca (Canada)	Amazon.co.uk (U.K.)
Amazon.com.au (Australia)	Amazon.fr (France)
Amazon.de (Germany)	Amazon.co.jp (Japan)
Amazon.com.mx (Mexico)	Amazon.es (Spain)

A 5-star rating *and* a short review (e.g. "Jam-packed with lessons on being FEARLESS!" or "Thoroughly enjoyed it!") would be much appreciated. We welcome longer, positive comments as well.

If you feel like this book should be rated at three stars or fewer, please hold off posting your comments on Amazon. Instead, please send your feedback directly to me (Jackie), so that we can use it to improve the next edition. We're committed to providing the best value to our customers and readers, and your thoughts can make that possible.

You can reach me at CustomerStrategyAcademy@gmail.com.

Thank you very much!

To your success and prosperity with a purpose,

Jackie Morey

Publisher-Collaborative Author
CustomerStrategyAcademy@gmail.com

www.ingramcontent.com/pod-product-compliance
Lightning Source LLC
LaVergne TN
LVHW041616070426
835507LV00008B/264